THE VIKINGS

THE
VIKINGS

——— ★ ———

by ELIZABETH JANEWAY

Illustrated by HENRY C. PITZ

Landmark
BOOKS

RANDOM HOUSE · NEW YORK

CONTENTS

Foreword

THE STORY OF HOW ERIC THE RED AND HIS SON LEIF sailed to the west and discovered Greenland and the continent of North America is a true story. I have tried to write a true book about their discoveries, but I want to tell you at once that not everything that you will read in this book is a *fact*. All the facts that we know about Eric and Leif and their voyages are here, but in between the facts I have put some fiction. I did not do this just to amuse you—or myself—or to make the book more exciting. I did it because the fictional parts of the book tell true things about the way people lived and acted and felt in Norway and Iceland and Greenland a thousand years ago.

For instance, you will find that in this book Leif Ericsson has a good friend named Brendan who is an Irish slave boy. Brendan is not a real character in the sense that Leif and Eric are. But when the Norse settled in Iceland they brought a great number of Irish slaves with them. Probably about a quarter of the population was Irish. Brendan, who is not real, represents the Irish in Iceland who were real. These Irish slaves were captured, just as Brendan and his mother were, in Viking raids and some of them were the sons and grandsons of petty Irish kings, like Brendan. Brendan is made up, but he is made up out of fact.

The other important thing in this book that is fiction is the duel that Leif fought in Norway. Again, this is made up out of fact to illustrate the way things were then. Many such duels were fought just the way I have described. Men like Leif always had to be ready to fight to hold on to what they owned. The Berserker that he fought is made up out of half a dozen descriptions in the Norse sagas of what these men were like and how they behaved. It was a violent age that Leif lived in, and the duel is there to show what the violence was like.

Now about the facts. You will find that most people in this country know very little about Eric and Leif, and that quite a few are inclined to believe that they did not really exist, and that Leif did not really discover America. These people say, first, that Leif could not possibly have crossed the Atlantic in a Viking ship without a compass or other aids to navigation. Well, the fact is that the Viking ships were at least as seaworthy as the caravels of the time of Columbus. In 1893 a Viking ship—that is, one built just like Leif's ship— sailed on her own from Bergen, Norway on April 30, and on July 12 came into New London, Conn. under sail without asking any help from anybody. She was about 80 feet long overall and carried a crew of about twelve men, all captains or first mates. This was a much longer crossing than Leif's. Leif sailed from Greenland to the southwest. He didn't have a compass, it is true, but he couldn't have missed the North American continent on that course no matter what he did, and the description of his first landfall is exactly what you find if you sail southwest from southern Greenland today.

The second question people ask about the Norse in America is—Why didn't they stay here if they really came? Why go back to gloomy, cold Greenland? The answer is simple. They couldn't stay because the Indians drove them out—and their own accounts say so. Remember, they didn't have any guns. When the Spanish and English and French and Dutch came to America five and six hundred years later, they had a hard time establishing settlements even with the great superiority over the natives that their weapons gave them. The Norse did not have that superiority. For some reason, probably because of a change in climate, there were no Eskimos in southern Greenland when the Norse settled there. All that Eric and his companions had to contend with in Greenland was a hard country and a hard climate. The Norse could overcome these things. But they could not settle and farm and raise cattle in a place where Indian arrows could threaten them at any time.

In telling you about the background of this book, I have used the word "saga" once or twice. The Icelandic sagas were the history books and the newspapers and the novels and the epic poetry of the old Norse people. "Saga" means "something that is said," and the sagas were originally memorized and repeated—but memorized and repeated in very exact form. About a hundred and fifty years after Leif's voyage (which took place just about the year 1000 A.D.), the sagas began to be written down. They were written as soon as people began to use the Latin alphabet instead of the old Norse runic letters which were not well suited to writing anything of any length. There are two main sagas about the discovery of America. One of them, scholars believe, was first made up in Greenland, though it comes from Iceland in the form we have it now. This saga is the best one to read for Leif's discoveries. The other was written in Iceland and is the best one for a description of the voyage to America that Thorfinn Karlsefni made some years after Leif's venture.

Perhaps you will wonder how a story could be repeated and kept straight for a hundred and fifty years before it was written down. There are several answers to this. The first is—practice. One of the things the Norse were skilled at and taught their children was just this ability to remember things straight and repeat them accurately. They had to. They did not have books to do their remembering for them, so had to keep things straight in their heads. Then, secondly, not having books or radios or television sets, they amused each other during the long dark winter days by telling over the stories they knew. Children would hear their grandmother's stories of sixty years back over and over again as they grew up, and would be able to repeat them word for word to their own grandchildren sixty years later. You see, life did not change fast in those days. If *you* tried to repeat your grandmother's stories today, you might easily get things wrong because you would be talking about an age that knew about horses and buggies but not about airplanes, an age without many things we take for granted now, when people acted and felt rather differently from the way we do. But in Iceland people lived and traveled and farmed and sailed the seas with very little change for the hundred and fifty years we are talking about.

Another reason why the sagas can be trusted is that the Norse people, although they were very democratic (both Iceland and Greenland were republics), were proud of the exploits of their ancestors. Suppose that a skald—that is, a man who made his living by remembering sagas and going about to people's farms and telling them—started to recite the saga which tells of Thorfinn Karlsefni's trip to America—and suppose he got something wrong. He couldn't tell the saga wrong many times before some member of his audience would get up and say something like, "Thorfinn Karlsefni was my great-grandfather, and that is *not* the way it happened. My grandmother told me it was thus-and-so." And he would set the skald right. Thirty-five men sailed with Leif to America and one hundred and sixty men and women with Karlsefni. Their grandchildren and great-grandchildren would all have had stories of the voyages handed down by word of mouth.

The facts in this book came from the sagas. In order to understand them properly I have read many other books by scholars, some of them based on the sagas and some of them the result of independent research. I have looked at photographs of the site of Eric's home in Greenland, and drawings of Viking swords and armor and shields that have been found by archaeologists. A whole Viking ship was buried in a grave mound in Norway at a place called Gokstaad and from photographs and descriptions of this ship, and others that were found in similar places, we know what the vessels of that day were like. Eric was a real person with a temper and a temperament just like what I have given him. He left Iceland under the circumstances I have set down. Leif was real. Not only his qualities of leadership and his strength, but even his extra-keen eyesight are described in the sagas. His brothers and sister were real and so was his mother, and it is quite true that she quarreled with Eric over becoming a Christian. Bjarni, who first sighted America, was real, and so were Thorhall and Tyrker and Gudrid and Karlsefni and the great king of Norway, Olaf Trygvesson, who was a friend of Leif's; and as for the polar bear cub, if Leif didn't take one to Norway, another Greenlander named Einar did later and made a great hit with the king by giving it to him as a present. Even some of the conversation in the book is right out of the sagas, and of course the voyages are as accurate as I could make them.

There are four people I want to thank for their help with this book. The first is my father, Charles H. Hall, naval architect and small-boat sailor, who supplied me with information on Viking ships, sailing boat voyages in Arctic ice, and navigation. In addition, many years ago he fostered my own passionate interest in the Vikings. Then I must thank Professor David Potter of Yale University who kindly helped me get the books I needed for research. My other two helpers were Mike and Bill Janeway. When they read the first Landmark books they told me I ought to write one. When I started to consider doing one, they nagged me to say yes. And when I began to write they listened carefully to the book as it went along, and made a number of helpful suggestions. Without them, it is fair to say, I never would have written this book at all. And I am awfully glad I did. I hope you enjoy reading it as much as I did writing it.

ELIZABETH JANEWAY

Redding Ridge
Connecticut

THE VIKINGS

CHAPTER I

Outlawed!

In the long light afternoon of a northern summer day nearly a thousand years ago, two
small boys sat on the stone wall which ran around
the barnyard of an Iceland farm. Behind them
rose a line of rugged hills, at the foot of which
nestled the farm buildings—a collection of low,
sod-covered houses, stables and barns. Below
them, across the road which was nothing but a rut-
ted track for the farm wagons, the land dropped
sharply to the steel-blue sea.

Sometimes the boys amused themselves by trying to throw pebbles down past the shore and into the waves which broke with a roar on the rocky beach. But today they were busy with another task. Light head and dark head were bent together over a piece of driftwood that lay between them.

"This will be a fine sword," said Leif. "When we get it done I will give it a name. I'll call it Tyrfing, after the great sword that the god Odin gave to his son. That's a good name, isn't it, Brendan?"

"A very good name," said Brendan, who was smoothing the blade of the sword with a piece of sandstone.

"And when my father comes home, I'll ask him to carve the name on it in runes," said Leif, who still hadn't learned to make his "runes," as the letters of the Icelandic alphabet were called. "Won't that be fine?"

"Fine."

"And then we'll make you a sword, and we can fight. Like real duels, with rules and everything. What will you call your sword, Brendan?"

Brendan raised his head and looked south across the bay. The wind lifted his short dark hair and he said, "I'm a slave, Leif. A thrall. How can I have a sword? Swords are only for free men."

"Don't talk like that!" Leif's eyes flashed with anger and he grasped more tightly the little knife with which he had been whittling the sword's hilt. "You are not a thrall—at least you will not be when I am grown and master of Haukadal! You and I are true foster-brothers, and we will be great champions together! We will go to Norway and see the King, and then we will go to Ireland and win back your mother's lands. You're no thrall, for you told me yourself that you were free-born in Ireland before your family was captured in a Viking raid."

"Oh, in Ireland!" said Brendan and laughed and shrugged. "In Ireland, so my mother says, my grandfather was a king himself, though not of a very large kingdom, I think."

"And you will be king again," said Leif positively. "You wait."

"I'll wait," said Brendan, "but in the meantime my mother is thrall to your father, and I shall not have a sword."

"You will if my father says you may," said Leif. "Won't you?"

Brendan smiled. "If Eric the Red says a thing is to be so, I think there are very few men to oppose him. Yes, Leif, if Eric says I'm to have a sword you may be sure I'll use it well."

"Then that's settled," said Leif, and fell to carving again.

Behind them in the barnyard a heavy-set brown dog jumped to his feet, sniffed the air, and ran across to the boys. Leif jumped up and stared down the road. Almost at once the boys heard a horse neigh and saw in the distance a little troop of men riding toward the farm, a cloud of dust blowing behind them.

"It's Father!" Leif cried, and turning toward the farmhouse he called, "Mother! Mother! Father's home!"

The door of the farmhouse opened and a tall woman in a long gray dress hurried out and stood shading her eyes, as she looked down the road. Other people joined her, some of them dressed in white, which was the mark of slaves. Leif, unable to wait, ran out with the dog, Helgi, at his heels and panted down the road to the oncoming troop of men. Sun glinted on spear points and sword hilts and steel helmets chased with silver.

Even on a short journey men did not ride without weapons in a land where safety depended on a strong arm and a swift stroke.

Quickly Leif reached the horsemen, and as he did so the foremost rode out well ahead of the others and stretched a big hand down to the boy.

"Holla, my son!" said Eric, laughing. "Quiet now, Wolf," he admonished his horse.

Leif put his foot on the toe of his father's spurred boot. In a moment he was swung up into the saddle before Eric, with the man's arm around him.

"Well now," said Eric, "this is a good greeting. Are you glad to see me?"

"Very glad," answered Leif as if his father should have known the answer to such a question.

"Then say hello properly to your friends who rode with me."

Leif grinned at the horsemen around him and said, "I give you greeting, Harald and Haakon and Thorstein and Bjarni—and oh, Bjarni, did you bring me the new little dagger you promised?"

"That I did," said Bjarni, "and two new tales to tell you beside of the Vikings from Jomsburg and their adventures."

"And you," said Eric, "have you had adventures this long week that I have been away? Have you behaved as an eldest son should? How is the baby?"

"Yes, oh yes," Leif replied. "The baby's fine. And Brendan and I are making a sword. It's to be called Tyrfing when it's done, and you'll carve the name on it, won't you, Father? And, oh Father——"

"What?" said Eric. He reined his horse up at the gateway. "Greetings to this house," he called loudly to the housefolk who stood waiting for him.

"May Brendan have a sword too?" Leif begged. "Please, Father. For he was free-born in Ireland, you know. Please. We want to practise sword-fighting together."

"Brendan?" said Eric, and his eyes sought out the dark-haired boy who stood beside the gate. "Yes," he said slowly and not smiling. "Brendan shall have a sword."

Leif bounced joyously. But Eric's eyes moved on to his wife and when they met hers he said, "We shall all need swords, I think, for I am this day proclaimed an outlaw!"

8

Outlawed or not, tired men who have ridden hard all day must eat and drink. Inside the big room of the main farmhouse fires were built on the stone floor for cooking and a keg of ale was tapped. But the bustle of preparation for the meal was subdued this evening and Thjodhild, Leif's mother, moved about her work in a silence that no one dared to break.

On the carved high seat Eric sat leaning his elbow on his knee and staring before him unblinking into the fire. His red hair glinted in the light and the heavy gold ring on his finger shone in the dancing flames. Beside him stood Leif, a very quiet Leif, whose heart was heavy with wondering what all this could mean. But he did not dare to ask his father.

At Eric's feet the brown dog Helgi slept, but in his sleep he growled once or twice and moved his feet as if he were chasing something.

Eric looked down at him and laughed, and Helgi woke up, raised his head, and blinked as if he were ashamed of himself. "Dreaming of rabbits, Helgi?" asked Eric. "In this country there are better things to hunt than rabbits. They hunt men sometimes, Helgi, men! But I never thought

Eric sat leaning his elbow on his knee

I would be one of the hunted. Still, I don't think it will be easy to catch me."

"They'll never catch you, Father!" Leif burst out. "Not while I live!"

"Leif?" Eric turned round. "I didn't know you were there. No, they won't catch me, son, and I thank you for your brave words. But brave words should come from a strong man, and you won't grow strong without supper. Go get a plate from your mother, now, and then ask Bjarni to tell you his stories, for he listened very carefully to get them straight for you. And be sure to thank him."

"Yes, Father." But Leif went slowly to where Bjarni sat, and he knew he wanted to ask the young man for a story different from Viking adventures.

"How did this come about?" he said, sitting down on the bench next to Bjarni.

Bjarni glanced at him quickly.

"I must know!" said Leif angrily. "I'm not a baby!"

"No," Bjarni agreed. "Very well, I'll tell you. Do you remember that early this spring a landslide crashed down on a house on the other side of the hills?"

"Of course I do. And the owner—Valthjof—

said that our thralls had done it, but they were just in the hills looking for new pastureland for the sheep. And—and he and his cousin Eyulf killed our men!"

"Yes," said Bjarni. "And then Eric called us out to revenge this deed, and Eyulf was killed in the fight."

"And he deserved it!" Leif exclaimed hotly. "Murdering unarmed thralls!"

"Yes," Bjarni agreed. "So I think, and so thought your father. But Eyulf was a free man and there is a penalty for killing a free man. Eyulf's relations brought their case before the court and they won."

"But that's not fair!"

"Fair or not, it happened two days ago, Leif," said Bjarni. "Your father is banished from Haukadal."

Leif stared about the firelit hall, where shields and weapons gleamed along the walls. He imagined how it would seem standing empty in days to come—unlit by fires through the long dark winter nights while the wind piled the snow on the roof and only a driven fox or two might creep in for shelter. He blinked to hold back the tears that were unbecoming a strong man. "What—what will my father do?" he whispered.

"Ah, if I knew all that was in Eric's head," said Bjarni, "I'd know more than I do now."

"But what will you do?" Leif asked.

"Oh," said Bjarni simply, "I'll follow Eric." He glanced at the boy beside him. "Now eat your supper," he said. "Then listen to a new story that I heard one evening when the court session was over from a far-traveled man named Gunnar Einarsson. Go on, eat, and when you're through you shall have your dagger."

So Leif ate his supper. When he was finished Bjarni drew from his belt a short dagger in a strong leather sheath. Leif pulled it out and his eyes sparkled. The hilt was ornamented with gold and the fine forging of the blade told of its strength and trueness. "Oh Bjarni," he cried, "it's beautiful! Thank you!"

"That's all right," said Bjarni, looking a little embarrassed. "There, go show it to Brendan. Eric wants me." His spurs jingled as he went across the stone floor to the group of men that was beginning to gather about their chief. On the bench Leif sat turning his dagger in his hands, even his father's outlawry forgotten for the moment.

He was roused shortly by his mother. She ran her hand over his hair and he looked up and smiled. "See, Mother? See what Bjarni brought me?" He held up the little weapon.

His mother looked down at it. "Yes," she said. "Blades for everyone, and fighting. Even for my little son."

Leif felt hurt. "I'm not little!" he said angrily.

But his mother just stroked his head again and said, "Your father wants everyone to sleep here in the hall tonight, where it is easy to keep a guard. I've brought you a cloak and you can tuck up right here on the bench."

Leif's eyes opened wide in excitement. "A guard!" he said. "Oh Mother, let me help!"

"You sleep," said Thjodhild. "That will be the best help. In the morning—in the morning there will be enough for everyone to do."

"Are we—going away?"

"Yes." She reached out and touched a great carved pillar that ran up to support the roof beam. "We must leave Haukadal now and find a new home." She bent down and kissed him. "Now go to sleep." He lay down on the bench and she covered him with the long woolen cloak she had brought.

"Mother," he said, rolling over to look up at her, "where are we going?"

"It's in this Northwest district only that your father is outlawed," Thjodhild told him. "We'll go south first, to our friends—Thorgrim and Thorbjorn Vifilson. Then—then we shall see. Perhaps we shall settle near them."

"Or perhaps we'll go to Norway?" Leif asked. "Perhaps to Ireland?"

"Perhaps." His mother nodded slowly.

"Brendan would like that. I must tell him. He says—Ireland is very green," Leif said as if he were talking to himself. "And there are great trees there. There are trees in Norway too. I'd like to see trees growing sometimes, not just scrubby little bushes like here in Iceland."

"You will see them. Soon, soon perhaps. Go to sleep now."

"All right." Beneath the cloak Leif felt for the hilt of his dagger and with that in his hand he fell asleep.

All night long Bjarni and Haakon and Harald and the rest of Eric's men took turns patrolling the yards outside, listening for the sound of horses' hoofs to warn them of approaching danger. And all night long Eric sat staring into the fire while the housefolk slept around him, planning, pondering, thinking of the lands where the Norse folk had settled, balancing this one against that. There were Norway and Ireland, England and the islands of the Hebrides and the Orkneys, where the long Viking ships lay in their harbors. The Norse had traveled to lands as far East as Russia where the great city of Novgorod had been built by the men from the North, and a Viking king ruled in Kiev. Eric thought of lands to the south, along the coast of Europe, past Spain and round into the Mediterranean where the Island of Sicily was a

Norse stronghold. Vikings had sailed to the very end of the inland sea, where they now guarded the Eastern Emperor himself in Byzantium.

At last, as the cocks crowed for dawn, Eric knew that his enemies would not come that night and he lay down and slept.

Next morning there was a great bustle. In those days a man of wealth—and Eric was a leader among men—could not put a checkbook and a roll of bills in his pocket and ride off. Gold rings, linked together, and coins from the southern lands where the Vikings plundered and traded might serve as money, but much wealth was in cattle, sheep and horses.

Eric proposed to leave nothing behind him to fall into the hands of his enemies. The cattle and sheep were gathered from pasture and stall and driven down to the water where a small but stout ship was pulled up to the beach to take them aboard.

Leif's mother and the baby were to travel in this ship south across the bay, or fiord, with most of the slaves. Spears and swords were placed under the after deck and beneath them two leather bags of gold and silver. Two of Eric's most trusted men traveled with Thjodhild to command the ship and bring her safe to the friends in the southern part of Iceland where the family planned first to take refuge.

Eric and the larger part of his band of men-at-arms planned to ride eastward round the head of the fiord with the horses and join Thjodhild in three or four days. Leif, of course, was to go with his mother.

Now this did not suit Leif at all. To sail south in safety, in the company of a lowing herd of cattle, seemed a very dull way for a boy who owned a dagger of his own to leave his home. So Leif sought out Brendan. While they hallooed at the cows to drive them out into the water where they could be hoisted aboard the ship, the two boys planned to vanish. It should not be a hard matter to hide until the ship should have cast off and be on her way.

They climbed aboard, accordingly, and jumped about the waist of the vessel. At last Haakon, in charge of loading the cattle, told them sternly to get out of the way—anywhere they wanted, in the name of the gods Thor and Odin, but out of the way! Then they slipped down into the water over the stern of the ship, and swam and waded ashore behind a tongue of rock that ran out into the bay. Dripping, they made their way back into the barnyard and hid under a pile of hay in one of the stables.

Eric was not pleased at all when, the ship safely beating out into deep water with slaves at the oars, the boys appeared. "You pair of imps!" he cried. "Your mother will think you're lost, Leif!"

"Oh, we left word," said Leif. "Brendan's little sister knows we're with you. She'll tell Mother."

"So I have to look after you," said Eric. "You're a nuisance. We have to ride hard."

"We'll look after ourselves, and we can ride hard, can't we, Brendan?" Brendan nodded vehemently.

"Come then, up with you," said Eric, making the best of things. The boys mounted two shaggy ponies and, in the center of the cavalcade, they started off.

It was too long a trip for the horses to be galloped, and the band of armed men and two wet boys rode at a bone-shaking jog-trot over the rough country. As soon as they were a fair distance from the farm, Eric struck inland away from the road they would be expected to follow.

In that northern country, right up under the Arctic Circle, the sun hardly set and it was not until ten at night that they halted. Up to that time they had stopped only to change horses or chew a bit of smoked meat. They were in wild country, and the mountains of the northwest peninsula of Iceland were still to their north.

The first night they camped in the ruins of a deserted farmhouse which had been burned down to its foundation stones. Eric looked about it grimly, thinking of what might await the home he had left behind. But he wasted little time on regret for what he could not help and soon, wrapped in his cloak, he slept beside the two exhausted boys.

Next day Leif could hardly stay awake in his saddle. His knees ached from gripping his pony, his teeth jolted together, he was sore all over. Brendan too was white under the tan of his skin. But the boys knew they must not delay the men in their push to safety out of this district. Here Eric's enemies could now attack him without fear since he was protected by no law.

"I must stay awake," Leif thought, "I must stay awake." He imagined himself pitching from his pony under the hoofs of the horses behind him, and he did not like the thought.

"Brendan," he gasped, "Brendan, are you sleepy?"

"Yes," said Brendan between his set teeth.

"We must talk to stay awake," said Leif.

"What shall we talk about?"

"Let's tell stories," said Leif. "I'll tell you— about the Jomsburg Vikings—as Bjarni told me." So, his sentences broken into short phrases by the jolting of their ride, he began the great saga of the band of men who ravaged the shores of the Baltic and set up a city where no woman could set foot, and where all the companions were sworn blood-brothers.

Then Brendan began, and through the afternoon he told Leif of the adventures of that Saint Brendan for whom he was named. Saint Brendan had set sail into the western sea in a skin boat, or coracle, such as the Irish still used. He had found fabulous countries, pillars of crystal set in the ocean, and an island that smoked and hurled fire out at the Saint and his friends.

Late in the afternoon Eric gave the word to swing south around the head of the bay. The cavalcade rode down out of the protecting hills, the men shook themselves alert and grasped their spears more tightly. When Leif saw his father loosen his sword in its sheath, he, too, put his hand on his dagger.

Eric stood up in his stirrups and peered ahead. "Do you see that line of hills?" he asked.

"Yes," said Leif.

"We are safe when we get there. At the foot runs a stream which marks the boundary of this Northwest district where I am outlawed. Across the river I am again a man under the protection of the law. So ride well now, boys, and we shall sleep in safety tonight."

"Assuming," said Bjarni, riding behind them, "that there is no one waiting at the ford to give us too warm a farewell."

Eric frowned. "Is there no other ford? This late in the summer the river is low. Where else can we cross, Bjarni? You know this country."

Bjarni reined up and thought. "We can try," he said. "We may have to swim the horses, but the river will be low. We should be able to do it now if we ever can. We must bear to the left, Eric, and look for a cairn of stones marking a burial mound. That is the place."

Eric gave the order, and the weary horses were spurred in the new direction. Everyone rode in silence now and, as it grew later, a faint slow dusk flooded the landscape.

"There," said Bjarni, in a whisper. Looking up, the boys saw a pile of stones heaped on top of a little hillock. "This is the place."

"Down to the river," said Eric. "Ride now. And if we must swim for it, slip off your pony, Leif, and you Brendan, and swim beside him with your hand on the bridle."

Quickly the men plunged down toward the stream. Leif, his heart pounding, thought that nothing had ever looked as sweet as the opposite bank, fringed with low scrub willow trees. The first man had all but reached the river when——

There was the twang of a bowstring and an arrow flew past him into the water!

"Stand!" cried a voice, and Leif saw two men on horseback ride from behind the little mound. "Eric the Red, you will pay for your bloody deeds!" cried the foremost of the men, and the

Swiftly Eric turned and, with a tremendous swee

...his arm, hurled his spear clear across the stream

other lifted a horn to his lips and started to blow a blast.

He never finished it. Quick as lightning, Bjarni's spear flew through the air and buried itself in his breast. The man coughed, threw up the hand which held the horn, and fell backward off his horse.

"Into the water, into the water!" cried Eric in a great voice, and with the flat of his drawn sword he beat Leif's pony on the flank so that the frightened beast leaped down the bank into the stream.

The man who was left spurred his rearing horse behind the mound and they heard him shout, "Come up, come up, they are trying to cross here!"

"Yes, and we'll do more than try," cried Eric. "They've left most of their men to guard the main ford. These are only two watchers. Steady, men! We'll make it!" But the ground was already thudding under the hoofs of horses.

Leif, peering back over his shoulder as his pony breasted the current of the river, saw a troop of men tearing up the bank, two or three times as many as Eric's men.

"Swim," cried Eric, "swim for it!" With the last of his band he spurred into the stream and slipped from his horse's back.

When the other horsemen reached the mound, Eric and his men were already finding footing on the opposite bank. "Ride," cried Eric. "They will not dare to cross after us. But their arrows can reach us here, and we cannot shoot back with wet bowstrings. Ride! The dusk is growing, and they will not see their marks for long!"

Leif scrambled onto his pony and, catching a long willow twig, he used it for a whip. Brendan was beside him, crying out to his pony in a strange tongue that Leif could not understand.

"Why it must be Irish Brendan is talking," Leif thought. "I must get him to teach me Irish,"—as if he had nothing else in the world to do but plan what he would like to study!

Over Leif's head an arrow rushed with a sound like tearing cloth and buried itself in the flank of a riderless horse. The horse screamed and ran frantically ahead, and Leif heard his father behind him cursing and calling on the Norse god Thor for help.

Swiftly Eric turned and, with a tremendous sweep of his arm, hurled his spear clear across the stream into the thick of the men clustered by the bank.

Then suddenly it was all over. Bjarni, in the lead, had found a small valley running up into the hills away from the river, and into this the men poured, thundered around a bend, and were safe from their enemies' arrows. Here they drew rein for a moment, and all that was to be heard was the sobbing breath of men and horses and Eric's voice, deep and soft.

"Hunted!" he was saying. "Hunted like rabbits! Never, never will I be hunted again! I call Thor to witness, I have never before run from a foe! Never will I be run and hunted like a rabbit again!" He drew a long breath between his teeth, his hand gripped his sword as if to raise it for a blow. Then he seemed to come to himself, slipped the sword back in its sheath and said, "Bjarni, how do we get through these hills? We must sleep far south of here, lest some of our friends try to slip over the river in the darkness and take back a dead man or two whom they can say they killed before we reached safety."

"This way, I think," said Bjarni, and in the dusk they rode after him.

CHAPTER II

Land to the West

TWO DAYS LATER THEY REACHED THE FARM OF
Thorbjorn Vifilson.

Leif, too tired to stand, slipped off his pony into
the arms of his mother who was laughing and
crying, kissing him and scolding him all at once.
Thorbjorn made a great feast for their welcome,
and invited Eric to spend the winter with him. Leif
was very pleased. He had never had so many boys

to play with in his life before. Besides, this southern part of Iceland was a more settled district than the Northwest peninsula. Neighbors were closer and there was going and coming all winter long.

Thorbjorn's son Einar was a bit suspicious of Brendan in the beginning—he said he was not used to playing with a slave-boy. Leif first explained that Brendan had been born free and captured in a Viking raid; and then, when Einar seemed still unimpressed, Leif challenged him to a wrestling bout and beat him. After that Einar said no more about Brendan being beneath him, and the boys ranged over the countryside together until the winter days grew too short. Then they practised wrestling and sword-fighting with wooden blades in the haylofts or, sitting by the fire, played checkers and listened to the stories of the visitors.

But if Leif was content, his mother was not. Thorbjorn was most hospitable, but Thjodhild missed her own home, and she was worried besides about the future. She hoped that her red-haired, high-tempered husband would settle in southern Iceland, but she was sure there were plans in his head for further adventures. Thorbjorn told Eric of an island out in the bay where no one lived now, and suggested that Eric set up a homestead there. But all Eric would say was that he would think it over.

However at the great midwinter feast of Yule, there was a visitor named Thorgest who knew this island—it was called Sudrey—and he told Eric it was a fine place. Moreover, the visitor said he was sailing to Northwest Iceland in the spring and he offered to stop at Eric's homestead there. He would take the house apart, and bring down the lumber so that Eric could build again on Sudrey island. Since no trees of any size grew on Iceland, it was always a difficult problem to find wood for pillars and housebeams. Eric finally accepted Thorgest's offer, and then Leif's mother was happier.

In the spring they all moved out to Sudrey and began to build stables and sheepfolds. Leif and Brendan took the sheep and cows out to pasture while the men worked and this gave them a fine opportunity to explore the island. They discovered a small sandy beach where they proposed to swim when it grew warm enough and a deep cave which they told no one about, keeping it for their own secret. But as the spring turned to summer Eric grew impatient, for Thorgest did not come with

the house timbers and Eric began to wonder whether they could be settled in their own home by the fall.

At last Eric could wait no longer and had himself rowed over to the mainland to see if he could get news of Thorgest. When he came back he was tight-lipped with anger. Thorgest, it seemed, had calmly taken Eric's property and was building himself a new house on his own farm! "Or he thinks he is," said Eric. "I am going to show him that he's wrong."

"Eric!" cried Leif's mother. "Not another fight! Oh wait, please wait! It's nearly time for the court session. Go there—Thorbjorn Vifilson will support you—and bring a case against Thorgest. That's better than fighting!"

"And where do we live this winter, then?" asked Eric. "In the cowbarn? Thorgest will have built his house by that time, and be in it. Do you think he's likely to help me tear it down again, move the timbers here, and rebuild before fall?

No, Thjodhild, we must catch him now."

"Eric, please! Thorbjorn will take us in again for the winter!"

But Eric only said, "I look after myself, and I need no man's help."

He took the stout small ship, in which Thjodhild had come across the bay from Haukadal the year before, and all his fighting men. This time Leif and Brendan had no chance to slip off with the men, for Eric told them to sit on a big rock by the sheepfold where they were under everyone's eyes. He threatened to tie them up like Helgi, the excited brown dog, if they moved.

So the two boys watched the ship take the waves, the sun gleaming on her striped square sail and on the row of shields along the gunwales. They strained their eyes after her as she moved down the bay and finally out of sight around a headland to the west. Then they had nothing to do but wait.

They waited three days. Leif thought they were the longest three days in his life. Brendan's mother Brigid went about her work with her lips moving constantly in prayer to the Christian God in Whom the Irish believed. Thjodhild, or the other hand, could only walk about as if she were in a dream. Once she asked the Irishwoman to tell about the Christian God, but she was too worried to listen, and stopped Brigid before she had got very far.

Then Eric came back. Brendan, who had been helping to cover the roof of the cowbarn with sods, saw the ship first and leapt down into the yard calling out, "There she is, there she is!" Thjod-hild ran down toward the landing beach. But Leif scrambled up on the barn to see for himself.

As the ship drew nearer they saw that she was low in the water. Lashed along the sides and across the waist of the vessel were the heavy housebeams that Eric had gone to get.

Leif gave a cry, "They've won, they've won!" And then he too scurried down to the beach.

Eric was standing on the ship's prow as the men,

having dropped the sail, rowed her in with the long oars they used close to land. "I've brought you your house," he called to Thjodhild.

But Thjodhild said, "What have you paid for it? How many men's lives?" Leif, beside her, was scanning the faces of the men at the oars, looking for the ones that were missing. Haakon—and a man from Norway called Olaf—and Bjarni——

Eric jumped down as the ship came up on the beach in the rush of a wave. He strode over to Thjodhild and took her shoulders in his two hands. "Everything must be paid for," he said. "Two men are dead and Bjarni is wounded. But Thorgest lost six for being a thief—his two sons and four others."

"Oh Eric——" said Thjodhild, and shut her eyes. "Now we will really be hunted—hunted out of Iceland by Thorgest and his friends."

"I only took back my property," said Eric.

"It wasn't worth it," said Thjodhild, so low that Leif could hardly hear her.

They brought Bjarni ashore with a wound in his thigh and a linen cloth stiff with blood wrapped around it. When they put him down on the beach he said, "Hello, Leif. Well, I didn't get to the hall of the dead heroes at Valhalla this time. I don't know whether I was too tough, or whether they're just overcrowded there right now."

"I'm glad—they're overcrowded," said Leif, and Bjarni laughed. But when Harald and Thorstein picked him up again to carry him to the farm, he fainted. Leif walked beside him up to the shed. There Harald and Thorstein laid him down on a pile of hay, but Thjodhild and Brigid sent Leif away before they began to dress Bjarni's wound.

Then began a curious time. Eric had sworn he would not be hunted again, but Thjodhild was right. Thorgest and his friends called a special court session. Although many men tried to help Eric's cause and testified that Thorgest had robbed him, Eric was declared in the wrong. As a result he was outlawed from all of Iceland for three years.

When this news was brought out to the island it was too late in the season for Eric and his family to brave the wintry seas. Eric's friends insisted that the family must not stay where Thorgest could find them and wreak vengeance for his two dead sons. So all winter long they moved about uneasily, staying at one farm for two weeks or a month, and

ERIC
the Red

moving to another friend's homestead before a rumor of their whereabouts could reach Thorgest.

Bjarni was sent home to his father Herjulf to recover from his wound, and Leif missed him. But Harald taught both the boys to run on skis that winter and every day while the light lasted they were out practising.

The one thing no one dared ask Eric was what they were going to do in the spring. The men-at-arms, who would rather have died than gone to serve some one else, were eager to set out on a voyage for trade and plunder down to England or the coast of France.

Leif and Brendan, who were sure they would be left behind with their mothers if Eric went a-viking, did not think much of this idea. Besides, from the little that Eric said they believed that he was anxious to leave Iceland altogether. He seemed to think that since justice had gone against him twice when he took the law into his own hands, he would never be able to live in peace again in Iceland.

But in what country would Eric settle? If he went to Norway, or Scotland, or Ireland, he would have to accept another man as overlord, a man who had settled there earlier. Leif could not imagine his father serving any overlord.

The boys were talking about it one afternoon when they came in from skiing. They had discussed half a dozen places when Leif said, "I wish your Saint Brendan had really found land to the west as the story you told me said he did."

Brendan bristled. "He did find land! You Norse believe that no one but yourselves can go exploring. Let me tell you, Leif, when the first Norsemen came to Iceland, they found the Irish here before them! Yes, it's true! The story of Floki of the Ravens says that when he landed here there were Irish hermits living in Iceland."

"Where did they vanish to, then?" asked Leif scornfully.

"They sailed to the west, to Brendan's islands, because they wouldn't stay here with heathens!" cried Brendan angrily.

"That's a lie!" Leif answered hotly, furious at being called a heathen. Promptly Brendan dived at his legs and bowled him over on the floor. In a second the two boys were pummeling each other to the accompaniment of such pleasant phrases as "Irish thrall!" and "Norse heathen!"

Suddenly a big hand came down on the shoulder of each boy and they were pulled apart. "What's all this row?" asked Eric sternly.

Leif was about to say, "He called me a heathen" —and then remembered that he had called Brendan a slave, which was at least as rude. "Noth— Nothing," he said and sniffled.

"Nothing?" said Eric. "What a fine thing to fight about! What will you do if you really disagree?"

"He said," Leif spluttered indignantly, "that the Irish came to Iceland before we did!"

Eric looked down at the boys thoughtfully. "He was quite right," he said. "Next time, Leif, you'd better try to find out the truth before you fight for pride in your own opinion. There were Irish priests here a hundred and more years ago, when the first Norse left Norway to escape the tyranny of Harald Fairhair. But when our people began to settle, the Irish wouldn't stay. No one knows where they went."

"Brendan does," said Leif bitterly. He didn't like being reproved even when he knew he was wrong.

"Oh?" said Eric. "Where did they go, Brendan?"

"They went west. They went to the islands Saint Brendan discovered in the west."

"That old tale!" said Leif.

"There is land to the west!" Brendan insisted. "I know it! I know!"

Eric sat down on the bench by the wall. "Come here, Brendan," he said. Brendan went over to him. "How do you know?" he asked, not challengingly, but as if he really wanted to hear.

Brendan stood before him and took a deep breath. "Two years ago the thrall named Svart told you there was good pasture in the mountains behind Haukadal. You remember?"

"I remember very well," said Eric. "That was the start of my troubles. I sent Svart and four other men out to look, and they never came back because Valthjof and Eyulf killed them."

"But Svart had been in the mountains before," Brendan told Eric. "He had been Valthjof's man once, before you bought him, and he had run away from him because Valthjof is a bad master. That's why Valthjof accused him of starting the landslide that ruined his house."

"That I didn't know," said Eric thoughtfully.

"No—Svart was afraid to tell that he had ever run away for fear that you wouldn't trust him. But it was only because Valthjof beat him. Anyway, he went up into the mountains one spring, and he was away nearly all the summer, living on berries and what birds he could snare and a rabbit or two. He wandered in the mountains for months, all over the peninsula. Finally, it began to be autumn, and he could find no more food and —well, he was caught, and returned to Valthjof. I suppose Valthjof would have killed him if he hadn't been short of men at harvest time."

Brendan paused, for he was coming to the important part of the story. Then he went on, "But about the land to the west—Svart saw it. If you go high enough in the western mountains, he said, you will see another range of mountains very far to the west, across the sea. There is snow on them even in summer."

Brendan stopped, as if he had run out of words. There was a long silence.

At last Eric stirred and spoke as if to himself. "Land to the west," he said. And then, "Gunn-bjorn saw land to the west, when he was blown out to sea rounding the west coast of Iceland." Then he fell silent again and the boys waited beside him, their eyes big, not daring to speak. Suddenly he shook himself and called, "Harald!"

The big blond man came over at once. "Yes, Eric?"

"Tomorrow," said Eric, "you will take your skis and go to Styr Thorgrimson's farm. There you will ask him how much he will take for the new ship he had built for himself in Norway. I want to buy it."

"Yes, Eric," said Harald.

"May I go with him?" Leif burst out.

Eric laughed, sounding merrier than he had in almost two years. "I don't know who has a better right to go, unless it's Brendan. You may both go—at least you may if you promise not to fight about nothing again along the way!"

CHAPTER III

The Voyage to Greenland

IN ANY COUNTRY OUTSIDE THE SCANDINAVIAN north at that time, people would have thought Eric the Red quite mad. He proposed sailing out over an unknown sea to look for a new country vaguely sighted once years before and vaguely confirmed by the word of a small boy and a dead slave.

Five hundred years later people were not slow to say that Christopher Columbus was mad when he set out to imitate America's first discoverers; and Columbus did not stow his entire household aboard one ship—wife, children, animals and all. Moreover he had, beside his own strong will and purpose, the backing of the King of Spain. He knew the use of the compass and of the first rough astronomical instruments.

Eric had no such help. He set his course by the sun in the daytime and the stars—particularly the Pleiades—at night; and by instinct. But behind that instinct lay not only his own ability and experience but that of his countrymen gained over hundreds of years. Julius Caesar tells of seeing just such double-ended ships as the Vikings used. Rock carvings in Scandinavia indicate that even in Caesar's time, Norse shipbuilding had a long history behind it. Many of the Norse ships, indeed, were bigger than those Columbus used. The famous Long Serpent which King Olaf Tryggvesson of Norway built just a few years after Eric's voyage to Greenland (and which Leif saw in Norway) carried almost a thousand men.

Eric's ship was smaller than that, of course, and built higher amidships for the rough Atlantic weather. She carried a big square sail worked by ropes of walrus hide. For breasting headwinds and coasting along the shore, oars could be run out through holes in the side that closed with little shutters when not in use. A heavy steering oar was fastened aft to the right, or starboard (steer-board) side. Eric's ship was decked over fore and aft, and over the open waist of the vessel a tent could be slung. She was about ninety feet long, and a carved dragon's head decorated with gilt was fixed to her bow.

So equipped, Eric set out. With him went forty stout men, his family, a few slaves, and as many of the farm animals as they could carry. Food for a voyage of several weeks was stowed aboard, but Eric planned to live mainly off the land he came to.

It was on a fine day in late May that his men rowed out into Breidafiord and then, as the wind reached them, hoisted the sail.

Three other ships, manned by his friends, sailed out to see Eric safe away from the vengeance of his enemies, and to bid him farewell. A long fare-well it would be, they knew, even if things went well. Possibly, almost probably, they might be looking their last on the big red-haired man who was determined to sail into the unknown. As the

Norse well knew, no man could escape the end which the fates had ordained for him. But this was no reason to fear! Rather it was a reason to leave behind a name and a reputation for adventure, for honor, and for courage.

As they came out into the open ocean Leif took his last look at Iceland over the stern where the dragon's tail of the ship reared itself high. His father's friends brought their ship about and cried out their goodbyes. Then they beat back to shore, where the tall cone of Mount Snaefel dominated the rocky land. Soon even their bright sails were lost to sight and only Snaefel looked out over the brooding sea. But the dragon ship set her prow firmly into the waves and with the wind behind her rushed away to the west, on the track of Saint Brendan.

That evening Leif had fresh milk from the cows aboard to drink, and a big bowl of porridge which he and Brendan ate together with carved horn spoons. Then they lay down among the sacks of provisions and the chests of household goods. Through the short night they slept to the tune of the rushing water and the wind in the rigging. And in the morning Snaefel was no longer there, and the ships drove through a waste of water.

So the days passed for almost a week. Sometimes Leif sat by the man at the steering oar to learn as much as he could of seamanship. At other times he watched how the men handled the sail to get the best of the wind and how Eric, at sunrise and sunset, took bearings to check his course.

In between times Leif and Brendan played with Helgi, gloomy at being tied under the foredeck and unable to chase the foolish chickens who squawked so near him. Tiring of that, they challenged each other to a regular tournament of checkers which they played on a little board set with pegs to hold the pieces still when the ship rolled.

Stories they told each other by the dozen and begged more from the men and from Brendan's mother Brigid who had a fund of Irish tales. But Leif missed Bjarni, who knew the best stories of all, but whose wound had not healed well enough for him to sail with Eric.

"When we grow up," Leif confided to Brendan, "we shall do things that will be told after us for years and years." Little did he think that he was already embarked on an adventure that would fire the hearts of men for ten centuries to come!

One morning Leif was wakened by a hoarse shout and lay blinking for a moment, wondering where he could be. The movement of the ship had just begun to tell him that he was at sea on a great adventure when the shout was repeated. Leif sat up. On the prow of the vessel stood Harald, his hands cupped about his eyes as he squinted across the bright sea. Men gathered about him, and in the stern Eric stood up by the steering oar.

"Land!" cried Harald again. "Land ahead!"

Leif couldn't see anything. "Let me see, let me see!" he shouted, making his way to the men about Harald. They let him through and he tugged at Harald's belt impatiently.

"Ahead to starboard," said Harald and picked the boy up. Following Harald's pointing finger Leif saw a line of snow-capped peaks glinting in the morning sun. Higher they reached than any mountains he could have imagined—high and cold and lonely. He drew in his breath. Here was land indeed—land to be conquered by strong men! How the waves must break on that rugged shore! Yet not for a moment did Leif doubt that his father could make a home for them there.

All that day they drew in closer to shore. But in the afternoon the wind dropped and fog came up and hid the nearing coastline.

"Out oars," cried Eric. "Let's sleep ashore tonight!" As the men swung the heavy sweeps the ship pressed stoutly on.

The fog was cold and growing colder. Leif wrapped a woolen cloak about himself before he went forward to the prow of the ship to join Thorstein, who had taken Harald's place as lookout.

In the silence of the fog the ship crept on, the oars creaking in the rowlocks. Suddenly——

"What's that?" cried Leif and just then Thorstein shouted——

"Ice! Ice! Keep her off!" Looming ahead through the mist, almost over them, was a towering mass of ice!

Swiftly thirty oars backed the ship away and the iceberg faded in the fog. "Sleep ashore tonight, will we, Eric?" called one of the men. "We're more likely to sleep at the bottom of the sea!"

"We won't sleep in either place," said Eric calmly. "We'll stand off shore till the fog lifts and we know where we are. Row out strongly. Nothing is won without a bit of a trial, lads. Remember the words of Odin's song——

> '*The unwise man*
> *Thinks he will live forever*
> *If he shuns fight,*
> *But old age gives him*
> *No peace*
> *Though spears may spare him.*' "

Eric pointed at the shore ahead. "We have something new to fight here instead of spears," he said, "but the song is still true. Across the sea we've come with a fair wind and found a new land. Are you going to cry now because it doesn't fall into our hands at once? Row out, row out! Tomorrow is a day too!"

But tomorrow, when it came, showed that Eric's landfall was not going to be quickly gained. All along that rocky coast a stretch of ice lay—not solid, but broken as the summer began to thaw it into a hungry pack of ice-blocks. Between these blocks, the strongest ship could be cracked as if she were a nutshell.

Again and again Eric ordered his men to the

oars as a lane of free water seemed to open and give promise of letting them ashore. Again and again the ice began to close in, and they had to fight their way out through the floating menace. Lucky it was that the stout Viking ship was built with a stern as sharp as her bow, and could be moved easily in either direction. And lucky it was that Eric of the keen eyes and the stout heart was in command.

At last even Eric gave up the attempt to land on this forbidding east coast of Greenland with its guardian demons of ice. It was clear that even if they got ashore safe they would never know when they could get out again.

So Eric gave the order to follow the coastline southward, standing well off shore from the ice-pack. For weeks, then, through cold and fog which darkened even the lengthening summer days, they beat to the south using the oars more often than the sail.

At length the land fell away and they saw a tall headland standing high above the sea. This they doubled cautiously, straining against the Greenland current which, driving to the south, still brings icebergs down along the Labrador coast.

Suddenly the ice was gone! Rugged mountains still ranged above them, but they were broken by deep bays on whose friendly shores the grass grew green.

Land at last! Now that it had been reached, Eric was choosy about where to set up camp. With breathtaking slowness—or so it seemed to Leif —the men rowed the ship in to the mouth of one of the fiords. Well forward stood Leif with Brendan by his side, watching the land grow nearer and take form.

"Look, look!" cried Brendan suddenly. "There are men swimming!"

Turning his eyes from the land, Leif saw a dozen dark heads in the water!

Behind them Eric laughed. "They're seals," he said. "Watch them dive. Even if men could swim in this cold water they couldn't stay under so long. No—there are no men here, no one to hunt or be hunted."

Then he was silent, peering ahead. At last he called back to the man at the helm, "That's an island to larboard. We'll land there."

The ship was too big to beach, nor did the rough shore look too inviting. Eric set her broadside onto the land and a small boat was lowered. Harald and Thorstein dropped down to take the oars and the boys tumbled hastily after them. Eric followed, and they rowed ashore.

"You first, Leif," said Eric as the boat grounded gently. "Step first on the land where you will grow up and hold your homestead when you are a man." And Leif leapt out onto the shore of Greenland.

He took two steps and promptly sat down. "The ground moves!" he cried. "I can't walk!"

Eric jumped ashore, laughing. "You've been at sea so long you've lost your land-legs," he said. "No, this good ground is solid. Eric's Island, we'll call it—Ericsey—and here we'll camp. There's good pasture for the cattle and sheep, and scrubwood aplenty to burn."

Then there was a bustle of landing indeed. The three small boats that Eric's ship carried plied steadily between ship and shore with men and cargo. Iron axes rang out as wood was cut for fires and for poles on which tents were pitched.

The cattle, too big for the boats to take, were forced over the side of the ship to swim ashore. Frightened and furious they lowed, coming up out of the cold waves, shaking their heads. The dog

Helgi broke loose, took a great leap over the gunwale, and swam ashore barking. On land, he gave himself a great shake that sent the water flying from his coat.

What a summer that was! Here was a whole new continent to be explored. Empty of men and barren it might seem, but men who had lived long in the Northwest of Iceland were used to barren prospects. The waters and the land were full of animal life—seals, walrus and narwhals, foxes and caribou which made fine eating.

Eric set part of his men to building shelters against the winter for themselves and the animals. Others gathered hay to heap in the low barns they constructed of stones and turf.

With his best hunters, Eric explored the mainland back to the great icecap that has not melted for thousands of years. Along the shore between the glaciers was land that an Icelander would know how to make fertile, and the hunting was magnificent. With him went the boys on shaggy Iceland ponies. Son of the Vikings and Irish slave alike felt themselves to be emperors of this vast new world.

When winter set in they went back to the is-

The waters and the land were full

animal life which made fine eating

land, well stocked now with hay for the animals and dried seal and caribou meat for the men. Their camp at the tip of Greenland lay actually farther south than the home they had left behind in Iceland and the sun stayed with them longer and returned sooner than there. Still, everyone was glad when the snow melted and spring returned and they were able to get about again.

Seeing that the ice left the fiord fairly early, Eric set some of his party to building a more comfortable home on the mainland. When the work was well begun he took the ship north along the coast. It seemed at first that the icecap would come down to the water's edge, leaving no foothold for men at all. But as they went farther north the glaciers retreated inland again, and Eric found other stretches of land for farming, and even richer hunting grounds. Here it was that they found the first polar bears, whose skins were to lie before their fires and cover them warmly during the long winter nights. And here it was that they made an even more exciting discovery—the traces of men!

It was a queer contraption of sewn skins ribbed with whalebone that they found first, and they might have puzzled over it for days if Brendan had not identified it.

"It's a skin boat!" he cried. "Just so—almost so—the Irish make them. Though it's very small. But—but—Leif, I told you Saint Brendan came here! It's an Irish skin boat! Sewn together with sinews, see, and the bones hold the shape."

"But I thought Irish coracles were almost round," Leif objected. "This is long and pointed and nearly covered over. See, there's just one hole here where a man sat, to row it."

"Well," said Brendan doggedly, "this is better for these rough waters. The Irish are a very clever people. They thought up this new design, of course!"

And though Leif argued that the boat looked more like something made by strange people native to this new land, nothing would shake Brendan in his belief that the Irish had settled in Greenland long before Eric came. When Thorstein found a little collection of ivory and bone needles and a comb, together with a stone axe, Brendan calmly claimed them as Irish too.

Constantly, as they explored the shore, Brendan

expected to find an old Irish hermit worshiping God next to the Arctic circle in the midst of eternal ice. He thought he had found one once and ran up to a big dark shape on the shore, crying out greetings in politest Gaelic. Just then the creature that Brendan had thought to be a hermit rolled over, scratched with a flipper, and fell into the water to reveal himself as a most respectable old walrus.

They spent that winter in the new house at Brattahlid and the next summer Eric explored minutely the neighborhood where he had first landed, working up the fiord and calculating how many families could support themselves on its shores.

By this time Leif and Brendan had grown quite out of all the clothes they had brought from Iceland. Their mothers spent the third winter weaving and sewing for them and for Leif's little brother. For in the spring they were going back to Iceland! Eric's period of outlawry was over.

At last, at last, the returning sun melted the ice! The water was ready to receive the ship which had slept through the winter cradled on shore like one of the cows in the barn. Over wooden rollers the

He revealed himself as a most respectable old walrus

ship crept into the water as if eager to leave the land behind.

Then came a busy loading for departure and the ship stood out to sea. Behind them southern Greenland fell back into its frozen slumber, no ringing axe to break the stillness, no cattle calling, no dog to bark, no boys' voices to shout from hill to hill.

Only in the far north the dark strange little Eskimo men plied their kayaks through the water after seal and hurled their harpoons at walrus and polar bear. They were ignorant still and would be for years to come of the tall fair invaders of their land. Greenland was empty again.

CHAPTER IV

A New Home—And
A New Land

BUT GREENLAND WOULD NOT BE EMPTY FOR LONG.
Eric planned to return, not alone, but with many
shiploads of colonists for the new country. It was
on the voyage to Iceland that he gave the new
land its name.

"Iceland," said he, "was a bad name. For years

after its discovery men hesitated to come to a place with such a forbidding name. But if we call the new country Greenland, now, people will be ready to come!"

Eric was right. The ship came quickly to Iceland with the news of their discovery and there were feasts made for them all through the Southwest. Everywhere he went Eric talked of fine empty land to be had for the taking, and family after family decided to follow him. Even Thjodhild, who had longed for home, warmed to the idea of settling permanently in Greenland since so many of her friends were going too.

As for Leif, Iceland already seemed strange, too crowded. He longed for the wild empty country to the west where he and Brendan had been monarchs of all they surveyed.

They spent part of the winter with Bjarni's father Herjulf. Leif had greatly looked forward to seeing his old friend but when they reached Herjulf's farm, it was to find Bjarni absent. He had sailed on a trading voyage and though they had hoped for his return in the fall, he did not come. Herjulf, listening to Eric's tales of free land and fine hunting, decided to join him in the

Greenland settlement, and began to lay in provisions and get ready a ship. Surely Bjarni would come to join them in the spring!

He did not, but when the Greenland flotilla set sail, there were twenty-five ships in it. Like American pioneers of eight hundred years later, the Norsemen were always ready to move on to new country where free men could live as they liked under no one's rule but their own. The unknown? It was nothing to fear! Danger? Hard living? They were used to such things. These were a necessary part of adventure and opportunity.

Setting out for Greenland again, Leif felt himself a veteran. It seemed they would have a pleasant friendly voyage with this crowd of ships.

But alas, the season that year was worse, much worse, than on their first sailing. The Greenland ice was thicker and lay much farther off shore, and there were storms. Two ships were lost in the ice. Another vanished on a night of wild wind and rain. Some of the more timid put about and hastened back to Iceland. When they rounded Cape Farewell, Greenland's southern tip, they had many fewer companions than when they had left Iceland. But stragglers came up in ones and twos, and fourteen ships in all won safe to the Greenland coast.

Now came the ritual of land-taking. By old Norse law, a man could take for himself no more land than he could pass over with fire in one day. That is, he was to light a fire as the sun rose, walk steadily through the day and light another as the sun set. Between the two fires his land would lie.

Eric had already laid claim to the fields about Brattahlid where he had built his house. Many settled nearby, up the fiord and on the shores of the next bay. Herjulf, however, chose a headland as far south as he could get, where he could look out to sea for the coming of his son. The old man was sure that Bjarni would follow him and Eric to Greenland.

Everyone worked hard that summer. There was no time for aimless roaming. More than five hundred people now lived on the land Eric's little band had found. Shelters must be built for them and their livestock before the coming of the bitter northern winter. Food must be laid in for man and beast.

Leif and Brendan helped drive the sheep up to mountainous pastures to preserve the grass close about Brattahlid for the winter hay. And at haying time, they worked like men through the long long northern summer days, sleeping in the fields at night—though it never grew really dark in the height of summer—and waking to work again.

Eric had brought with him a famous huntsman named Thorhall. With a small band that tough and rather hard-bitten gentleman set out to kill everything he could find that would be useful for meat or fur. The boys longed to go with him, but Eric would not let them, lest they slow down the men who were hunting not for sport but for the means of life itself.

At last as the days grew shorter and the nights longer the work slackened and everyone began to prepare for the harvest feast. Although Leif looked forward to the celebration, he was worried, too. The ship of his friend Bjarni had not yet rounded the headland where Herjulf had built his house. Surely Bjarni with his stories and good humor would come! Surely he was too fine a sailor to have timidly turned back from the Greenland voyage!

No, Bjarni had not turned back. On the very night of the feast, when many neighbors had gathered at Eric's house, Leif heard a stamping of horses outside and ran to the door to see who these late guests might be. It was dark and the firelight could only penetrate far enough to show him that several men had ridden up and were dismounting.

"Who's there?" he called.

"Who wants to know?" a voice answered from the dark.

"Leif Ericsson. Who's that?"

"Leif Ericsson? But he's a little boy," the voice teased. "You're too big to be Leif Ericsson!"

"Bjarni, Bjarni, you've come!" Leif shot out of the door as if he'd been catapulted from it. "Bjarni!"

"Yes, it's Bjarni!" The man laughed. "But is this really Leif?" He hugged the boy and pretended that he could not lift him into the air. "Why you're a foot taller than you ought to be! You can't be Leif. And besides, you haven't asked what I've brought you! Leif always asks that."

"Oh Bjarni—was I really so rude, those years ago in Iceland? I don't care whether you've brought me anything or not! At least—Bjarni, I know you've brought a new story!"

"Oh, I've brought a fine story, you can be sure of

that. But I won't tell it out here in the freezing dark. Ask Herjulf and me in to the fire, Leif, and I'll tell you a story such as you never heard before."

"Come in, come in. But Bjarni, just tell me what the story's about, won't you please?"

"Why it's about my adventures, of course," said Bjarni. "What else? For I've been clear over the edge of the world, Leif, and I've seen a new land! A land such as the King of Norway would tear his hair out by the handful to own!"

"No!" cried Leif. "Bjarni, tell!"

But Leif had to be patient. Eric and Thjodhild, overjoyed to see Bjarni again, made him welcome. His old companions clustered around and it wasn't until after everyone had eaten and drunk their fill that Bjarni could begin his tale.

"I missed your sailing from Iceland by a month," he said, "and I can tell you I wasn't pleased to find you'd gone off without waiting for me. So I decided to follow along."

At this, it seemed, his men had been even less pleased than Bjarni. They wanted to sell the cargo they'd brought from Europe and enjoy themselves. Bjarni told them they could stay behind if they liked, but they'd get no profit from the cargo unless they went with him. After a few bitter wrangles most of the men decided to go. Joined by a few others who had been too late to sail in the ships of the Greenland flotilla, they set out.

The storms that had harassed Eric's fleet descended on Bjarni too. Fighting headwinds, it took them three days to get out of sight of Iceland. Then fog closed down, hiding the sun. Storms rolled them about until they had no idea where they were.

The men grumbled at their bad luck and cursed Bjarni for a mad man and themselves as fools. But at last they got a glimpse of the sun and, since they had a favoring wind, they sailed on for Greenland. And they kept on sailing. Bjarni scratched his head in puzzlement. Where were they getting to? They should have reached Greenland long ago —but he decided they might have been blown far to the east during the storms and fog, and held on his course.

Then they saw land—and it wasn't Greenland! Bjarni and his men gaped at it. Where were the cloud-piercing mountains of ice that should mark their landfall? Wooded and low, this land stretched north and south as far as the eye could see.

"Was there good hunting?" cried out Thorhall the huntsman, interested only in his own specialty.

"I didn't land," said Bjarni.

"Didn't land?" Thorhall was stunned.

"If I landed that crew," said Bjarni grimly, "I thought I'd never get them to sea again. No, I didn't land. I was on my way to Greenland, wasn't I? I knew this wasn't Greenland."

But Thorhall could only mutter over Bjarni's lost opportunity.

Bjarni had turned the ship away. The woods and the absence of ice made it clear that he was hundreds of miles too far south. He stood out to sea in a northeasterly direction and sailed on for two days more. Then—land again, still wooded and low! Bjarni was beginning to think he was enchanted and sailing in circles. Less than ever was he ready to land, and he held his grumbling crew off shore and stood away once more.

Three days passed and—there was land again! This time Bjarni was a bit encouraged. Hills were beginning to rise, and the land was more barren.

They were obviously getting closer to their goal. On they went—four days more with a strong southwest wind behind them—and the Greenland coast, unmistakable, was before them.

"Here we are at last," said Bjarni, relieved, and sailed in to land—at his own father's farm!

As Bjarni finished, his hearers sat silent pondering for a moment on this strange tale. Then Bjarni was engulfed in a wave of questions. Was the land rich? Had it seemed good for farming and cattle? How tall were the trees? Tall enough for ship-timbers and keels? Had he seen any men? Any animals? What about harbors? Rivers? Were the fish plentiful? Faster and faster the questions flew until Bjarni looked desperately at Eric for help.

"Wait, wait," cried Eric. "Let him catch his breath. And remember, friends, we have one country to be settled here before we go on to another!"

In the silence that followed only Brendan's voice was heard. "So that's where the Irish went," he said thoughtfully.

"Oh, you and your Irish!" cried Leif, half laughing and half impatient. "Will you go back next summer, Bjarni?"

Bjarni threw out his arms and stretched and

yawned. "Why Leif, it comes into my head," said he, "that the land won't run away. As Eric says, there's much to be done here and I've a fancy to stay ashore awhile. When you're grown I'll lend you my ship—for she knows the way now—and you and your Irish friend can go looking for his countrymen."

"I'll hold you to that," said Leif.

CHAPTER V

Leif's First Voyage

So many years before a boy grows up! It seemed to Leif as if they would never pass. The Greenland colony prospered and grew, though some seasons were bad and hunger was not unknown at the end of a long winter. Another little brother and a sister came to live at Brattahlid and the house was enlarged and made more comfortable.

During several summers Leif and Brendan went to the northern hunting grounds with Thorhall.

There they learned the art of hunting with bow and arrow and with spear, and how to set traps. They found the nests of eider ducks and collected the precious down that lined them. They learned to capture the cold-eyed Greenland falcons that kings and earls through all of Europe were beginning to declare the finest in the world. During the winter they learned from Eric how to form the strange runic letters of the Norse alphabet. And they both grew tall and strong, though Leif outtopped his friend by half a head.

At last it seemed to Leif that it was time for him to set out upon his adventures. He was a man grown, and his brothers were old enough to help Eric run the farm. So he went to his father and asked for a ship.

Eric rubbed his graying head. "So soon?" he said. "You're still a child."

But Leif only laughed.

Eric peered at him shrewdly. "I was wrong," he said. "A child would have been angry. I see you are a man, Leif. But you must let me think. Where do you want to go?"

"West," said Leif after a moment. "West, where Bjarni went."

"So Greenland is not enough for you, Leif?"

"Was Iceland enough for you?" Leif asked his father.

"I was not exactly pressed to stay there, if you remember!" Eric replied. "It's different for you. I am the first man in all Greenland, and you will be the chief after I die. That should be enough."

But Leif was silent.

Eric sighed. "Well, I will think."

Two days later he called Leif to him. "Do you still want to go adventuring?" he asked.

"I'd hardly forget about it in two days," said Leif.

"I'll give you a ship, but on one condition."

"What's that?" Leif asked.

"That you sail not west, but east," was Eric's answer.

"East?"

"To Norway."

Leif looked his question.

"To Norway," said Eric firmly. "I would have you take gifts to this new king. He is powerful, very powerful, this Olaf Tryggvesson. I would not have him forget us who live here on the edge of the world, or remember us unkindly. We are beyond his reach, no doubt. But I would like to make sure, just the same, that no man coming from Iceland will try to dispute our claim to Greenland. Go to Norway, Leif, and make it clear to the King and all his court that we hold Greenland! But that, holding Greenland, we are his friends. Can you do this?"

"I can try," said Leif slowly.

"Besides," his father went on, "it won't do you any harm to see how they live there in the narrow land your grandfather left, where I was born. You'll find some things good—they live more easily there—and some things bad. We have no beggars in Greenland, where each man knows his own worth! Go and see it, Leif, and see the King. I've taught you what an educated man should know, or your mother and I and your friend Bjarni have between us. Do this before you sail off into the wilderness."

"I'll do it," said Leif. "But then I will sail west."

"All right," Eric agreed. "Then you will sail west."

Eric gave Leif the ship in which he had first explored Greenland. They had talked of this voyage first early in the year, but there was a great deal of work to be done in preparation for the trip. In the middle of June Leif was still loading cargo in the fiord below Brattahlid. First of all the finest skins, the stoutest walrus hides and strongest ropes made of hide, must be selected to take to Norway for sale in the King's new market town of Nidaros. Thorhall the Hunter and Eric picked over hundreds of skins that spring, rejecting most, selecting only the thickest and softest of fox, marten, and seal skins.

Then, when Leif was nearing the end of his patience, Eric had a new idea. Leif's gifts to the King must be the richest, the most wonderful, that Greenland could provide. Of course there would be a pair of Greenland falcons, trained for the sport of hawking by Eric himself. But this was not enough. Eric determined to send the King something unique, beyond price, something never seen in Norway—a polar bear!

Leif raged when he learned that Thorhall had gone north to find a bear for the King. The season was late enough as it was for the long voyage to Norway.

"I'll finish loading and sail whether Thorhall is

back or not," Leif told his father, and pressed his men to finish their work.

But Thorhall returned with a day or two to spare. With him, he had a small, white, playful little object who stood up on his hind legs and licked at Leif's hand when Thorhall brought him aboard. It was a bear-cub for the King.

So they got off. They went not by way of Iceland, but on a more southerly course that took them past the Orkney Islands which lie north of Scotland. Here Norsemen had first raided and then settled, building their great halls on the larger islands and setting out from the harbors in their dragon ships for voyages of trade and plunder. And here, it is said, Leif met a girl named Thorgunna whose face never quite went out of his head again, and gave her a ring——

But he had a mission to accomplish. In the fall he sailed his ship into Nidaros (now called Trondheim) which King Olaf Tryggvesson had made his chief city. With him Leif had a pilot from the Orkneys who knew the Norwegian coast, for the sea approach to Nidaros was nothing to undertake without knowledge. But the shoals were safely passed at last and Leif and Brendan, full of the pilot's talk and gossip, found themselves staring at the King's city. A sparkling river flowed through it, and behind it were hills clothed in the thick Norwegian forest.

Leif couldn't take his eyes away from the scene. "Trees," he said, "such trees! Think of it, Brendan. To live where it is always green! Where fuel for fire can be had anywhere by swinging an axe—not put together from peat and turf and cowdung and driftwood and scrub birches and willows no higher than my head! What a rich, rich land this Norway must be! The King will dazzle our eyes with his jewels and gold!"

"Yes," said Brendan, "but remember, Leif, we have walked where he never set foot, we have seen sights no man in Norway has looked on."

The little bear, grown larger now, lumbered across the deck (they could not bear to cage the friendly creature), and reared himself up by Brendan to have his head scratched. The pilot, who had been standing near them, hastily drew away. These young men from the end of the world spoke nicely enough and seemed to have the manners of gentlemen, but why—the pilot wondered—did they let

that wild animal roam about threatening everyone? In Scotland men kept dogs for pets! He
had some kind of an idea that in Greenland such
a habit was looked on as too soft, and that nothing tamer than a wolf or a bear was regarded as
a fitting pet.

It would be hard to say just where the pilot had
got that idea—but Brendan, at any rate, had done
nothing to deny it. Neither had he tried to correct
the pilot's belief that, while they ate cooked meat
in company, Greenlanders at home always pre-
ferred it raw.

Leif looked after him now and laughed. "He
thinks we're savages."

"Let him," said Brendan. "As savages, Leif,
we'll be noticed. If they think us savages, any manners and knowledge we possess will seem remarka-
ble. But if they expect polished manners from us,
they'll see only where we fall below the level of
the King's court."

Leif nodded. There was wisdom in Brendan's
words. "They'll dazzle us with jewels surely,"
Brendan went on. "If we'd brought gold to give,
all our hoard would mean nothing to the King compared with his own wealth. But think how clever

Eric was! We do not bring gold, which every man who seeks the King tries to offer. We bring what no one else can give, the gifts of Greenland herself, furs and falcons and that fat foolish little bear. Why, of course we're savages bearing savage gifts! If we were not, it might take us a month to see the King, but as savages, mark my words, we shall see him, one way or another, before two days are gone!"

"Gentlemen," said the pilot, approaching Leif again but on the side away from the bear, "I have brought you safe to Nidaros, have I not?"

"That you have," said Leif. "And now you would like your wages. Will you take them in gold?"

"Well," said the man, "if you want—but Nidaros is a trading town, you know, and I'm not a bad trader. If I could have eight of those white fox skins, now——"

"Oh," asked Brendan, "are white fox skins common trade goods in Nidaros?"

"Not common, but much sought after. I'll do better with those than with gold."

"I see," said Leif and grinned at Brendan. "You shall have them, then."

"Not eight," Brendan said hastily. "Six is enough."

"Another trader!" said Leif. "No, eight. Let him tell his friends here that men from the end of the world may be savages, but they are generous savages. Six you get for being a good pilot, and two more for friendship and for the tales you have told us. Why without him, Brendan, you'd never have known that King Olaf's second wife was an Irish princess! Give him the skins and see that he is put safe ashore."

"Blessings on your generous heart!" cried the pilot, and went off with Brendan to get his pay.

Leif wanted to go ashore at once, but Brendan persuaded him to wait a day until news of their coming should have been spread about the town by the talkative pilot. The boat which set him ashore brought back fresh food and they feasted on the ship that night with many a toast drunk in thankfulness for their safe voyage.

For the first time Leif and Brendan sampled a favorite drink of the Norsemen called mead, which was made from honey. No bees lived in the northern climate of Greenland or Iceland and such honey as was imported there was all used for sweetening, for sugar was unknown. Leif and Brendan found their heads reeling very soon from this potent drink and were thankful that they had tried it in private, and not at the King's court!

They slept late the next day and it was nearly noon when they left the ship. They were dressed in their best—long tight trousers of woven stuff, short tunics traced with embroidery in gold and silver thread, and gold belts about their waists. Beside his sword, Leif wore at his belt the dagger which Bjarni had given him so many years before, on the day his father had first been outlawed.

Three men went with them, carrying some of their finest skins. A hooded falcon rode on Brendan's wrist, and the little bear wore a red leather collar and trotted at Leif's heels, led by a silver chain.

They landed at the market which lay along the shore for the convenience of the trading ships that put in there. As they stepped from the ship's boat, a hush fell over that noisy, crowded place and more men than Leif ever remembered seeing together turned to stare at them.

"It's the Greenlanders! The Greenlanders!" voices whispered, and Leif felt suddenly homesick

LEIF
the
LUCKY

for the empty, lofty mountains of his own lonesome land. At his feet, the little bear whimpered in fright.

"Why come now," said Leif to the bear—and to himself, but only he knew that—"what a foolish baby you are! This is Norway you've come to, and you're going to see the King. Has any other bear from Greenland had such an adventure?"

The little bear looked up at him, stood on his hind legs, and licked his hand. Then they walked across the market place to the hall of the King.

It was the biggest building that Leif had ever seen and it dominated the town of Nidaros. Before it, the paved courtyard was thronged with groups of men-at-arms, house-servants of the King, and adventurers lately landed in Nidaros from the ends of the earth.

Here were bronzed men who had fought the Moslems beneath the Mediterranean sun, or guarded the Byzantine Emperor in Constantinople. Here were men who had raided up the Seine to the city of Paris, and men who had been with King Olaf when he laid siege to London. He would have captured it too, but for the English archers on London Bridge who held his ships off. It was his suc-cessor Saint Olaf who took London and tumbled down London Bridge, as children a thousand years later still sing. And now here were the Greenland-ers, swinging across the courtyard with their heads high.

About the carved doors of the great hall clus-tered a group of beggars, blind or lame, some dis-playing unpleasant sores and moaning for alms. At the approach of the newcomers they surged for-ward, holding out their hands. The tallest of them muttered something in Gaelic and caught at Bren-dan's cloak. The little bear was frightened and Leif picked him up and held him on his shoulder, and at the sight the beggars fell back.

Leif gazed at the pitiful mass of humanity and then his eyes passed on to the noble carving on the doorway which reared to twice a man's height. What a contrast there was between the beautiful art of the doorway and the broken beggars whining for help in half a dozen languages!

"In all of Greenland," Leif said thoughtfully, "there is no such work of art—and there are no beg-gars either. Little bear, you and I have much to learn of the ways of men in Norway! Brendan, give these poor folk a handful of silver." Then they passed into the hall.

It took them a while, standing by the doorway, to adjust their eyes to the smoky darkness of the interior, for even the King's palace boasted no window glass in those days. It was lighted only by small windows covered with animal membrane. The smoke from the cooking fires, moreover, was allowed to find its own way out through holes in the roof instead of being drawn up in chimneys.

But the enormous room—it must have been two hundred feet long and sixty wide—was hung all about with tapestries. Its floor was strewn with rushes and sweet-smelling herbs.

Leif and Brendan looked at the King's high seat—but it was empty. The King was not there.

A tall man with a broken nose had been watching them. As Leif and Brendan stood looking around the hall he came up with a companion, a fat, rather greasy fellow, and lounged between them and the door. Leif felt their eyes upon him, but he scorned to stare back.

At last the man spoke. His voice, like his nose, seemed to have been damaged somehow and never set right, for it was husky and hoarse. "Are they just animal trainers, think you, Klaus," he said, "or do they juggle, too?"

"I doubt they have the skill to juggle," answered Klaus. "More likely the dark one who looks like an Irishman carries a pair of dice whose special tricks he knows. Perhaps the big blond one pretends to be an honest player, and gets others to play by seeming to win."

Brendan's voice cut through. "Did you know that in Norway, Leif, insects spoke the language of men?"

"This I would not have believed," said Leif. "King Olaf must have been too busy with his wars lately to have noticed what has crept in through the cracks in his palace walls. It's a good thing we have come here, Brendan, for in our land such few insects as there are we know how to crush between our finger and thumb."

"What is your land, juggler?" asked the broken-nosed man.

"Insects—and vermin," said Brendan cheerfully, ignoring him. "Methinks we've brought the wrong beasts, Leif. Greenland bears and falcons prey on noble creatures. We should have brought ferrets and terriers, such animals as a farmer uses to clear rats and lizards out of his barns."

"I'll kill you, Irishman!" said Broken-nose venomously.

"Did some one speak?" asked Brendan. "Or was it just a mongrel cur growling that I heard?"

"Just a cur," said Leif. He beckoned to the men who had come with them from the ship and handed the bear to one. Then he loosened his sword in its sheath. Brendan took off his leather hawking glove and one of their companions slipped it on and took the falcon, and Brendan's cloak.

"The King is not here," Brendan said. "When he returns, no doubt he'll have the hall swept out. When it's clean we'll come back. Meantime, let's go."

He and Leif moved side by side to the door. Broken-nose and fat Klaus gave ground before them. Just as the four reached the courtyard where the beggars waited, Broken-nose suddenly swung himself before Leif, trying to trip him up. But Leif, in the long Greenland winters, had had skillful teachers in the art of wrestling. He avoided the man's rush, caught his arm and, apparently with no effort at all, turned him over in a somersault on to the ground before him. Broken-nose lay on his back with the wind knocked out of him.

Fat Klaus at once set up a howl. "Guards, guards, seize these men! They're brawling in the King's hall itself! Ho, guards!"

Leif looked at Brendan. It seemed as if Broken-nose and Klaus had succeeded in trapping them! From the beginning, no doubt they had intended by their insults to provoke Leif and Brendan into fighting. To get them arrested was part of the plan.

Brendan caught Leif's arm. "It's all right," he said. "Leave it to me. I think we may have friends here you don't know about."

Two huge men in link armor and steel helmets came up. "What's all this?" said one.

Broken-nose obliged by rolling on the ground in apparent agony. "They tried to break my back," he moaned.

The guards didn't look very impressed. Still, they had their job to do. "Is that true?" said one to Leif.

"I'll be happy to break his back," said Leif, "here or anywhere that the law permits it. Is it usual for strangers come to visit the King to be first insulted and then tripped up as they walk through the palace doorway?"

"He tried to trip you?" asked the guard.

"Liars! Liars!" screamed Broken-nose. "Ask honest Klaus there what happened—how the big one took me by the shoulder and threw me down. Ask all these honest men too," and he gestured at the beggars.

The guard looked from Leif to Broken-nose and back. "Klaus no one will believe," said he, "for you two are closer than the sword and the scabbard. But the beggars should know." He looked at them inquiringly.

Klaus nodded at them. "Speak now, and tell the truth," he said. And it occurred to Leif that he sounded very sure of himself. After all, how easy it would be for these poor beggars to be bribed!

Leif stared at them and felt that their eyes hesitated to meet his own. He was suddenly stricken with anger at himself for falling into such a stupid trap before he had even seen the King! Obviously, Klaus and Broken-nose planned to get the Greenlanders held by the guard and then offer to vanish or to withdraw the charges if Leif and Brendan would pay them enough. The whole plan flashed through his head in a second as he waited for the beggars to speak.

Brendan spoke first. "Aye lads, speak up and tell the truth!" And then, looking straight at the tallest beggar, who had only one arm and one eye, he added some words in Gaelic. They were spoken so quickly that Leif, who knew a little of the language, could not follow.

But the tall beggar understood! Leif could see his eye widen and suddenly his twisted face broke into a smile. "Brother and countryman," he said in Gaelic, "I *will* tell the truth, then!" He went on in Norse: "The man on the ground there tried to trip up the tall blond fellow, but that one knows his wrestling. He sent him over on his back with one hand. Then the little fat one started to shout."

"Is that so?" the guards asked the other beggars.

"That's so," they all agreed, once the tall one-eyed beggar had spoken.

"You rats!" Broken-nose sat up, forgetting all about his back. "You've been bribed!"

"Not by us," said Leif.

"That's enough, Ketil," said the guard to Broken-nose. "We know you've made trouble before. Get out, now."

"Get out, is it?" Broken-nose, or Ketil, glared at the men around him. Fat Klaus was already edging away from the group. Ketil's breath came fast, his teeth ground together, he trembled not with fear but with rage. Suddenly he leaned forward and roared at Leif, "I challenge you! I challenge you to duel with me, to holmganga! Thirty times has my sword Leg-biter tasted human flesh. From Upsala to Dublin am I known! I challenge you, I challenge you, I, Ketil the Berserker! Do you dare to fight me, you Greenland coward?"

Ketil's berserk rage had come over him so fast that Leif was stunned. He had heard of the Berserkers of course, who could drive themselves into states of fury before battles or duels and fought as if no weapon could touch them. However, he had never seen it happen before, though his father's huntsman Thorhall had the reputation of having been a Berserker in his youth. For a moment he could only stare at Ketil.

"The man's mad!" said Brendan. He turned to

the guards. "My friend's done him no wrong! Why should he have to fight this fellow?"

The guards shrugged. "He has a right to challenge anyone he wants. Of course your friend doesn't have to fight."

"Coward, coward," roared Ketil. "I challenge you! Your property against mine! Fight, or make over your ship to me!"

Brendan stared aghast. He had expected the talkative pilot to announce their arrival to everyone in Nidaros—but who could have expected such harm to result from the man's gossip? More than likely, Ketil had been waiting for them at the King's hall ever since the pilot's story reached his ear.

"That's what he's after," one of the guards explained. "He's fought duels before for property. We know him. But—the law says he may. We can't stop him."

"Then the law's as mad as he is!" said Brendan.

Leif laughed, and the sound rang out across the courtyard as if it came from a different world from Ketil's hoarse roars. "Brendan!" Leif laughed. "You said *we* were the savages in Norway! Why, we've had to come two months' sail from Greenland, from the end of the world, to find out what savagery is! Nothing in Greenland is as wild or cruel or untamed as this mad dog!"

"Fight, fight!" Ketil howled.

"Fight, fight!" Leif mimicked him. He was angry now too. "Why you poor fool, I'll kill you! Fight! Do you really want to fight me, who keeps bears as other men keep cats? Who wrestled with a walrus when he was ten years old and swam three times around an iceberg? My father and my grandfather before me left settled lands for killing men who bothered them! And you challenge me!"

At this fat Klaus disappeared completely, but Ketil was beside himself and could only scream, "Fight, fight!"

"We'll fight then," said Leif, having recovered his temper and feeling rather ashamed of himself for losing it. "Fix the place, Brendan, and ask the guards to come and witness fair play." He took his little bear in his arms and walked off stroking it.

Ketil's roars ceased and Brendan thought for a moment he was going to back down, but the thought of Leif's richly laden ship was too much for him. Sullenly he agreed to fight the next day.

CHAPTER VI

A Fight and a Stranger

Now THE RULES OF SINGLE-COMBAT FORMAL
duels, or holmganga, were many and complicated.
Originally the duels were fought on some tiny
island, barely more than a rock, so that the oppo-
nents could not get away from each other. Later,
somewhat the same narrow boundaries were kept
by laying out a cloak on a field and pegging the
corners down. About the cloak a square area was

marked off and the combatants fought within it. If either stepped outside with both feet he was held to have fled, and to have forfeited the fight.

The fighter who first shed blood on the cloak could put a stop to the duel, but then he lost. If neither surrendered, the one more severely wounded was held to be the loser. The swords of the fighters had to be the same length. Each man was allowed to use three shields, but when the third had been broken, or cut to pieces, he had to stand on the cloak and defend himself only with his sword.

This kind of sword-fighting Leif and Brendan had often practised together and Bjarni, Eric, and Thorhall had all given the young men lessons as they grew up. But Leif had never fought in a real serious duel before, while ugly angry Ketil had ranged Norway, Sweden and the Western Isles making his living by challenging other men to fight. When they lost, as they usually did, he claimed their property.

Ketil was one of a whole class of landless men who lived by violence, too restless and ambitious to attach himself to one master and do his bidding. Such men, and most of the Berserk fighters were of this kind, were a worse pest to Scandinavia than "outlaws" like Eric, who had broken a law but never the code of honorable behavior. In the end, only twelve years or so later, the right of a man to fight another for his property became so abused that it was made illegal.

But that time was still twelve years off on the misty morning when Leif and Brendan, with a dozen of their shipmates, set out to the dueling field. Ketil was nowhere to be seen, but the two big guards were waiting and Fat Klaus was talking to a group of hungry-looking fellows.

The guards called Brendan and Klaus and proceeded to lay out the field for fighting. Leif turned his back on them. He could trust Brendan to see that all was done right.

Leif wanted to think not of the coming fight, but of what he was fighting for. He was fighting, in a way, for all of Greenland. He represented Greenland here, and all its people. Their way of life had been challenged. It was rough and crude, no doubt, but never cruel and savage and dishonorable as were Ketil and his kind. Leif's father had sent him to the King to make sure that Greenland could live in freedom, ruled by its inhabitants. If he lost his fight to the worst elements in Norway, he would lose any chance to win the King to his father's way of thinking.

Leif drew a deep breath and shut his eyes. Suddenly, against his eyelids, it was as if he saw the outline of the mountains behind Brattahlid take form. For a moment he seemed to sniff the Greenland wind, keen and clean off a thousand miles of ice!

There was a noise behind him. He swung about. Ketil was swaggering across the field to the men who were laying out the dueling ground.

"Make it small, make it small," he shouted. "Give the coward no chance to run!"

"We'll make it the right official size," said one of the guards coldly.

Ketil paid no attention. "Ahoo!" he roared, threw back his head, and began to shake. He was working himself up into his Berserk rage. He drew his sword and made it ring against his shield and then held it to his ear. "Where is my guardian?" he muttered. "Where is my guardian? Are you there, Wolf? Are you there?" Then he howled again and announced that his guardian wolf was with him.

Leif felt the hair rise along the back of his neck

Now they were really fighting!

as he looked at Ketil, making his own filthy magic for his own gain. Disgust and contempt mingled within him, but knew he could afford to give way to neither. Of course the Berserkers' fury did not protect them from wounds, but it really did protect them to some extent from *feeling* their wounds. It was as if they put themselves into trances and dulled their sense of pain so that they could go on fighting long after other men would have been forced to yield by agony and loss of blood.

Brendan came across to Leif with Klaus. The duelists' swords were measured together and proved to be the same length. Then each man with his first shield stepped forward on to the cloak.

"Leif Ericsson strikes first!" called the guardsmen. "He was challenged."

This isn't real, Leif was thinking, this can't be happening! But he drew his eyes away from Ketil's grimacing face and aimed a shrewd blow at his legs. Quick as a flash Ketil's shield went down and Leif's sword rang on the metal rim. The noise restored him to himself. It was real—and he had wasted the first blow by doing what Ketil had expected.

Now they were really fighting! Ketil, panting and roaring, waded in toward Leif, crowding him

off the cloak, trying to push him out of the dueling square by sheer weight of blows.

While Leif ducked and parried Ketil's attack, he
thought quickly. Ketil had the advantage of mad
fury. But he, Leif, had the advantage of a clear
head. He let Ketil drive him almost to the edge of
the square and then—he ducked swiftly under Ketil's sword and sped behind him!

In his mad rush Ketil could not stop and before
he had realized that Leif was no longer in front of
him, he himself had placed one foot outside the
square.

"He flees, he flees!" cried Brendan.

"It was one foot only," the guardsmen answered.
"Let the fight go on."

Ketil swung about, but as he did so he turned the
wrong way and exposed his sword arm instead of
keeping his shield between Leif and himself. Leif
swung almost quickly enough. His blade nicked
Ketil's shoulder, but did not disable him.

If Ketil's roars had been frightening before,
they were awe-inspiring now! Again he closed in
on Leif, and again Leif was reduced to parrying
blows with his shield. At last the shield gave way.

Ketil's blade bit through and Leif knew it had tasted blood in his forearm.

"Another shield!" he cried.

In a moment Brendan had given it to him. But Leif, as well as Ketil, was wounded now, and he had used up one of his shields. The haze of battle descended upon him. Ketil's nimble legs were his mark. They bore evidence of many fights before. So with shield high, Leif thrust low, low, trying to cripple Ketil. He ruined Ketil's shield, but he did not even nick him. Still he fought stubbornly on. Dust rose, making a cloud around the two fighters. Then Leif's second shield broke, and he felt Ketil's blade in his side.

"It's nothing," he gasped to Brendan, who was bringing him his last shield.

"He's tiring," Brendan said. "Fight shrewdly, now!"

But Leif could see no evidence that his opponent was tiring. Blood from Ketil's wound soaked his sword arm, but he handled his weapon as strongly as ever. Alone, alone in a dust cloud with a madman, Leif fought on for the honor of Greenland. Ketil was calling now on the old bloody god Tyr for victory. Oh Eric, my father, thought Leif,

Eric help me now! How can I defeat this wolf-man?

Why, by being a man! It was as if Eric's voice had spoken in his ear, and with it Leif caught again the tang of that clean wild Greenland air. Use your head, he seemed to hear Eric say. Change your tactics. You may not have fought wolf-men before, but you've fought wolves and worse beasts too. Outthink him, Leif, with your man's brains!

Slowly Leif gave ground before Ketil, as he had before. Too furious to be wary, Ketil came on in another mad rush. Again Leif dodged around him, taking Ketil's blow on his shield, but this time he swung his own blade sooner and his sword bit deep, deep into Ketil's shoulder. And well that it did, too, for Leif's last shield flew to pieces on his arm!

Ketil took two steps, his eyes fixed, his lips frothing—and fell straight forward onto the ground, outside the dueling area. Even if he could rise to fight again, he had stepped past the bounds and lost the fight!

Brendan, his shipmates, and the guards raised a great shout. Fat Klaus had turned and was running away, leaving his friend to bleed to death.

The scene swam and shimmered before Leif's eyes, for he too had lost blood aplenty. He felt Brendan's arm round him, supporting him. "Bind up—the fellow's wound," he gasped, "else he'll die. Show him we savages—fight fair." Then it seemed to him as if darkness came down over the scene, and he knew no more.

When he came to himself he didn't know where he was. It was dark. He lay in a little room lit by a candle. He was stretched full-length on a bed, covered with fur robes. Tapestries shielded the walls. Leif recognized the woven scenes as portraying the Saga of the Volsungs. Just above the bed, Sigurd slew the dragon Fafnir. Leif felt a deep sympathy with him, as if he too had slain a dragon. Then he remembered the fight and tried to sit up to see where he was.

"Lie down!" a deep voice said. "Would you burst your wound and start it bleeding again?"

Leif did as he was bid. It was the kind of a voice that you obeyed. Out of the shadows by the door a tall man came forward. The candle threw its flickering light on his face. Leif had never seen him before.

"Where am I?" Leif asked haltingly.

"In the palace," the tall man said. "The guards brought you here."

"That was kind. But I'd rather be on my own ship."

"Perhaps you would. But the doctor would rather have you here. So here you'll stay till you're cured."

Leif thought this over and decided he would wait to argue about it till he felt stronger. "And Ketil?" he said.

"He's here too, but not in such comfortable quarters. He'll live, unfortunately. But probably not to fight again."

"That's fine," said Leif.

"Are you hungry?" the tall man asked.

"Starving."

"I'll have them bring you some soup."

"Soup!" Leif exclaimed. "I want roast meat!"

"But soup is what you'll have." The man laughed. "Is every one in Greenland so given to argument as you?"

"And is everyone in Norway so given to having his own way as you?"

The man's eyebrows drew together in a sudden

frown. But in a moment his face cleared and he burst into a laugh. "That's a good one! Is everyone in Norway so given——" he broke off to laugh again. "No, Leif Ericsson, you're quite right. No one in Norway is so given to having his own way as I am! Now rest, and I'll send you your soup and your friend." He went out, still laughing.

Leif couldn't understand what he'd said that was so funny, and lay puzzling over it till Brendan came in.

"Well, what did you think of him?" asked Brendan.

"The man who was here? But who is he, Brendan?"

"Who is he! By the voyages of Saint Brendan, Leif, didn't you know him? That was Olaf Tryggvesson himself!"

"The King!" Leif shot up in bed and then lay down quickly as he felt the pain of his wound. "By the hammer of Thor! And I told him he liked his own way too much!"

"Oh Leif, Leif," cried Brendan. "And they say we Irish are the talkers!"

CHAPTER VII

Leif the Lucky

LEIF'S OUTSPOKENNESS, HOWEVER, SERVED ONLY
to endear him to the King. When Olaf came again
to visit him the next day, he gave clear evidence
of his liking for the young Greenlander, and invited him and Brendan to spend the winter with
him.

Leif found it easy enough to lead the conversation round to the position of Greenland, and the
King readily confirmed Eric's claim to the land.

He was delighted with the little bear and so pleased with the falcons that he told Leif he must send him more by the first ship that sailed from Greenland for Norway after Leif's return.

In the evenings Olaf enjoyed having Brendan sing him the sad Irish airs that his Irish princess, now dead, had taught him.

"Your friend is a Christian," he said to Leif one day.

"Yes. The Irish——"

"——are not the only Christians." said Olaf. "I am one myself, as you may have heard."

Leif tried not to smile at this understatement. Olaf was not merely a Christian, he had vowed to convert all the Northern lands to his faith. The report was that his method of conversion was to send missionaries to a district one year, and to follow them up with an army the next, which army was to "persuade" those who hadn't yielded to the missionaries' preaching.

"I have heard that you are," Leif said.

"And you?"

Leif was silent. This man had been kind to him, and more than kind. But Leif was not a Christian, nor could he lie about it to the King.

"Are you a pagan?" the King went on.

"Not that either," Leif said slowly. "I am not—I cannot believe in the fairy stories about Odin and Thor and Loki that I learned when I was a child. I believe—well, so far I have believed in my own strong arm."

"And is that belief enough?" the King asked. "In your fight with Ketil did you wish for no other aid than your own strength?"

Leif remembered how, sore-pressed, he had appealed to the image of his father. He told this to the King.

The King smiled. "He helped you, then. But we Christians also appeal to Our Father, Leif, and He has very often helped us when no human father could. Think of it."

"I will think," said Leif.

Olaf stood up. "I have confirmed you in your title to Greenland—if, indeed, the Norwegian King can do so. I will not go back on my word. You and your father hold Greenland whether you turn Christian or not, and I'm not likely to send anyone to find out whether you worship Christ or Thor at the end of the world. But I am fond of you, Leif. I would like to see you a Christian. And if I have done anything for which you feel grateful, I would like to ask you, in return, to carry two priests to Greenland, so that Brendan and his countrymen may have the comfort of their religion. Will you think about that, also?"

"Of course," said Leif. He did think, too, during the months of that winter which by Christian reckoning began the year 1000. He thought while he and Brendan followed the King in his hunts, visited Olaf's fleet in its winter quarters, and sat about the fire listening to the poets sing of the deeds of Olaf and his forefathers.

One of the things Leif remembered was Brendan's mother's calm faith in the face of strain and danger, and Brendan's own laughing courage. Christianity had been reckoned a slave's religion in Iceland, since only Irish slaves believed in it. But it was ceasing to seem so now to Leif, and to many others.

In the end, he not only agreed to take the two priests to Greenland when he sailed in the spring, but he was baptized a Christian himself. The only worry he had was over Eric—he wished he had had a chance to tell his father first. But that was out of the question.

Spring came on quickly, and soon it was time to sail for home. The furs Leif brought with him had been traded for Norwegian goods—precious iron, wheat, honey, and all the things that Greenlanders had to import or do without. One day as they were loading the ship Brendan came to Leif.

"The King has asked you to take two passengers," he said.

"Yes, the priests," said Leif.

"I'd like you to ask him if you can take two more."

"Two more priests?" asked Leif, puzzled.

"No, no," said Brendan. "Two more passengers."

"But who?"

"Well——" Brendan paused. "Does the King know of your plan to explore the land Bjarni found?"

"No, I've never talked to anyone about it," Leif replied. "Better to find it first, I think, so people won't think we're talking nonsense."

"Tell him, Leif, and then ask him to give you the two passengers I want to take."

"But who are they?"

"They're Irish runners," Brendan answered.

"A man and a girl. They're the real wild Irish from the western isles, captured a year or so ago in a raid. They can run—they can run fifty miles a day, Leif, for three or four days. They'll be eyes and ears for us in exploring a new country. They're used like sheep dogs here, and no one speaks their language. I've talked to them. They'd be happy to come with us and they'd be worth their weight in gold."

"What are their names?" Leif asked.

"Haki and Hekja. Will you talk to the King?"

"Today."

That evening Leif brought the subject up. The King's eyes opened wide as Leif told him of Bjarni's adventures and of how he wanted to sail west from Greenland.

When Leif finished, the King said, "So there is land past even the end of the world!"

"We think so," Leif said. "We plan to go and see."

"Good luck to you, then. Of course you shall have the Irish runners. And when you come back you will send me word of all you find."

Leif promised, little knowing that within a year Olaf Tryggvesson would have been slain in a bloody sea battle with Olaf of Sweden and Sven Forkbeard of Denmark.

The runners were sent aboard and Leif and Brendan set sail for Greenland just a year after they had left home. They had an uneventful trip, landing their cargo safely at Brattahlid in August.

Eric was rejoiced at his son's safe return with news of King Olaf's friendship. Lest he appear womanly, he hid his pleasure and pride in Leif's accomplishment behind a good many gruff remarks about the arrival of the priests. He was much too old to change his religion, he claimed, and beside he had no desire to go to the kind of Christian heaven which the priests described to him. A tough old fighter, he had looked forward all his days to spending eternity in the Hall of Heroes at Valhalla. Here, the Norsemen believed, the souls of those who died bravely were brought by Valkyrie maidens, to spend their days in fighting and their nights in feasting.

When Thjodhild, his wife, became a Christian Eric wouldn't speak to her for a month. At the end of that time he discovered that Thjodhild wouldn't speak to *him*. Then his roars of fury against the priests were terrible to hear, until Leif managed to make peace between his parents. Leif's successful voyage to Norway had already won him the name of Leif the Lucky. Eric declared that his son's good luck was at least matched by the misfortune he had brought back with him to Greenland in the shape of the priests!

But Leif, who knew that his father's bark was worse than his bite, cheerfully ignored Eric's anger. Beside, he was much too busy preparing for the journey to the west. Bjarni had been in southern Norway and came home soon after Leif, and Leif was with him constantly, learning all Bjarni could tell him of the land he had glimpsed and how to get there. They agreed that Leif should use Bjarni's ship. Neither Leif nor Bjarni was superstitious enough to believe that Leif would have an easier time finding land to the west because his ship had been there before—but both knew that Leif's crew might very well find comfort in the idea that the ship "knew the way."

As spring drew close and Leif engaged his men— thirty-five sailed with him—Eric's grumblings ceased. He talked often with Leif about his trip, and finally Leif realized that his father was longing to go too! "Come with me, then," he said. "They may call me lucky this year, but you are the best-known captain, and your luck has been proved by the settlement of Greenland."

"No," said Eric stubbornly. "This is your venture. I'm too old, I'm too old." And he sighed.

"Nonsense! Of course you'll come. The men will be delighted to sail under your command."

"No, no," Eric protested. But in the end he gave in.

Then he broke his ankle! Once he knew he really couldn't go, he roared with rage. The horse that had stumbled and thrown him as he rode down to the ship, he cursed by all the gods in the Norse mythology.

"You're killing me!" he howled at Thjodhild as she attempted to bandage his ankle. "But what does it matter, I'm done for anyway. Oh, for a man like me to die in his bed like a coward!"

No one could handle him except an old friend of his youth, a German named Tyrker, who had lately come to Greenland. Leif remembered Tyrker from the Iceland days. He had loved him dearly when he was a small boy, and he was deeply grateful to him now as the two of them finally quieted

Eric enough for Thjodhild to get her bandaging done.

When she had finished Eric lay in bed and looked at Leif. "So it's true," he said. "I'm an old man. I've said it often enough, but I never really believed it."

"Breaking an ankle," said Tyrker drily, "is hardly a disease of old age."

"Lying in bed with it is," said Eric. "Twenty years ago I'd have been on a horse again—but not that misbegotten, bewitched he-devil!—and riding down to sail within an hour. What a horse! What a piece of luck!" He closed his eyes and groaned. "Well, Leif, now it's up to you and that Irish slave-boy."

Eric had made Brendan a free man some ten years before, but it did not seem the right time to remind him of it. "We'll do our best," Leif said.

"Young puppies," Eric responded unkindly. "Tyrker, you'd better go in my place."

"I'll be glad to," said Tyrker, "if Leif wants me."

Eric growled. "I know you. You're saying that to humor me. You've decided to stay here and play checkers with me to keep me quiet while the boys go off and get into trouble. I won't have it!" he roared at the top of his lungs. "You go with them, Tyrker, or they don't sail! You go with them and bring them back safe!"

"But Father," Leif said, "Tyrker will be a comfort to you here while you're laid up."

"It'll be more of a comfort to me to know he's looking after you. What's the matter? Don't you think I'm man enough to be patient for a few weeks while they nurse me? Don't you?" Actually Leif didn't, but he didn't want to say so. "Well," Eric went on, "I will be. Have I ever broken my word, Leif?"

"No."

"I give you my word that I'll make no trouble. Will you accept that?"

Leif said, "Yes."

"Now I give you an order," Eric said. "It's the last order I'll ever give you for I know you're a man grown. But I know, too, that an older man who's seen much of the world can be valuable to you. Take Tyrker with you."

"Yes, Father."

"All right. Now go. Don't delay your sailing while you have a fair wind. Tell your mother I've given my word to lie here like a hulk and to do whatever she says. Goodbye, my son, and good luck to you."

"Goodbye," said Leif and clasped his father's hand.

Eric blinked as if there were tears in his eyes. He crushed Leif's hand in his own. "But tell your mother," he shouted, "that if she lets those priests in here I'll get up out of bed, ankle or no ankle, and chase them out! Mind you tell her now!" As the door closed behind Leif and Tyrker he was still roaring.

CHAPTER VIII

To the West!

To FIND THE LAND THAT BJARNI HAD SEEN, LEIF reversed his sailing directions. That is, Bjarni had touched last at a barren northern land and then come, with a strong southwest wind behind him, in four days to Greenland. So Leif made for the southwest. Behind him the coastline began to disappear as, once before, the coast of Iceland had vanished.

How like, and how unlike, that childhood voyage with his father was this! Then Leif had sailed into the unknown with the simple faith that since his father was in command nothing could go wrong. Now it was he who commanded, he who was responsible for the men who sailed with him.

After they had sailed five days—a day longer than Bjarni—and still seen no land, it did occur to Leif that Bjarni had once thought he was enchanted. Leif sat up in the dark—it was night, and Tyrker had relieved him at the steering oar—and thought about this. There *was* something a little magical about Bjarni's story. He had seen three lands, and three is always the magic number in a fairy tale. Bjarni had got home safe, but Bjarni had not set foot on shore.

Leif was grown-up, he was commander of an expedition, he knew that as a Christian he should be beyond the reach of old, evil magic. But just the same, he felt a sudden shiver up the spine. Everyone had always believed that Greenland lay at the end of the world and that past it there could only be enchanted isles. Where were they going? Or—was there really nothing there? Had Bjarni seen not land, but mirage? Half-sitting in the dark, Leif thought about this. He wished he could talk to someone about it, but he knew he could not. Not even to Brendan. Not even to Tyrker. He was the commander. He must not show his doubts to *anyone*.

Slowly he lay down again. Bjarni had said that he ran before an unusually strong wind on the last leg of his journey. His ship must have daily covered a good many more miles than the average day's sail, which was the unit by which the Norsemen measured their trips. That was why they had not yet seen land. Leif repeated this to himself until daylight. Then he sat up and peered ahead. There was nothing there.

When land was sighted at last, the next afternoon, it was in the most matter-of-fact way that could be imagined. Leif was asleep. He'd had two wakeful nights. Brendan was at the helm. Tyrker was sitting next to him, and to amuse himself and Brendan on the long monotonous sail, Tyrker was rolling dice, left-hand against right-hand. The left hand was for Brendan, the right for Tyrker. They were pretending to bet on the dice, and the stakes had got rather high. Tyrker had supposedly just lost the city of Dublin, a gold drinking-horn and two ships the size of the Long Serpent, and was

grumbling about it. He accused Brendan of deliberately letting the ship roll more when it was Tyrker's throw.

"Well," said Brendan, "take the oar and I'll roll for you instead of you for me."

"I'm an old man," said Tyrker, "but I've never heard such a brazen attempt to get me to do your work for you. It's your watch at the oar. You needn't think I'll take it for—What's that?" He stood up, stuffing the dice in his pocket.

Brendan stood up too. "Land," he said. They both looked ahead at an uneven line like a low cloud along the horizon.

"Shall I wake Leif?" said Tyrker.

"Let him sleep," Brendan answered. "He's been worrying at night because we didn't make our landfall. Sit down, now. I'll bet you the kingdom my grandfather lost, God rest his soul, against that gold brooch of yours that I can roll a seven before you can." They went on playing.

When Leif woke up two hours later the coastline was distinct, and Brendan had reduced Tyrker to an imaginary state of beggary and was threatening to sell him to the Emperor of Germany for his debts.

"Good afternoon, Captain," Brendan said to Leif, when the latter rolled over and stretched. "Would you like to take the helm as we come in to land?"

"Land?" Leif sat up. "Why didn't you wake me?"

"Because I knew you'd wake up yourself," said Brendan calmly. Leif, looking ahead, ignored him. He almost couldn't believe it. He'd looked so often——"It's there, all right," said Brendan.

"I see it is," said Leif. All doubts, all worries dropped away, and Leif became the commander. "Keep the oar, Brendan. Tyrker, have the men make a small boat ready and then come forward to me."

He strode up to the prow of the ship through the groups of men who, having stared their fill at the land ahead, had now gone back to eating, whittling, playing games and telling stories. Ahead, to the west, the land grew steadily clearer.

It was barren land. Bjarni had said so, but Leif thought he had never seen anything quite so useless. The ground was covered with large flat stones and in the distance a glacier glittered in the sun. Leif, Brendan, and Tyrker spent a day on shore, and no one could think of a reason for spending another.

"Well, we landed," said Leif. "It's more than Bjarni did. But I can't say it's much more." He kicked one of the stones. "Helluland—Stoneland," he said. "Let's go back to the ship." So they rowed out.

"Now what do we do?" Brendan asked.

"Coast the land south, of course. We don't know whether Bjarni's landfalls were islands or a mainland. We must see whether they are joined together."

So, through the height of summer, they sailed south, using the oars when they had to, keeping the land on their right hand. Not knowing the shore, they did not keep too close, and at night they anchored. The nights were fairly short, though longer than summer nights in Greenland. They were definitely working into a new climate.

After some days the character of the land began to change. One fair morning Leif rowed in again, to a white sandy beach, where thick woods came down to the sea.

"Now this is a land!" cried Brendan leaping ashore. "Look at the timber, Leif! We can fell enough trees here to make our fortunes twice over when we sell them in Greenland!"

"That we can," Leif agreed. "And yet, Brendan, I think we'll sail on. We can return here on the way home if we want. But let's sail to the south while the good weather lasts. Bjarni saw three lands. Let's not go home having seen less!" Brendan and Tyrker agreed and they returned to the ship. This country Leif called Markland, or Wooded-land.

Again they coasted the shore. It is likely that

Sometimes Leif went with the explorers

they came down between Newfoundland and the mainland of Canada through the Strait of Belle Isle. At one time, crossing the Gulf of Saint Lawrence, they seemed to be out in the open ocean again. But they picked up the shore again after two days. Following it, they marveled at its richness, at the enormous trees that stood above the long white sandy beaches of what we now call New England.

At last, one perfect summer day, Leif determined to land and make camp. He had decided to pass the winter in this new country, and he wanted time to build shelters, gather food, and explore the land around about.

In the early morning, just as the sun rose, they steered the ship close in. The peaceful ocean broke gently on the sandy beach of a little island, and Leif told the men they could anchor and go ashore. They ran about on the beach laughing and wrestling together playfully, for they had been confined for weeks to the ship. After the stale water they'd been drinking, the dew on the grass tasted as sweet as honey.

The island was too small to winter on, however, and soon they went back to the ship and sailed it into a sound which lay between the island and the mainland. The tide ran out surprisingly fast—Leif had never seen such swift tide—and since the bay was shallow, the ship ran aground! A fine captain I am! Leif thought to himself, surveying the tidal flats about the ship. He had never done such a stupid thing before. But Tyrker laughed him out of his shamed feeling. No harm was done after all, for Viking ships were built for beaching, and the rising tide would float them again.

The men were so eager to be on shore that Leif let them wade across the sand to where he could see a river emptying into the bay. They came back to report a lake lying up the river. It was a perfectly protected anchorage, and when the tide rose they rowed the ship up the river and into the lake which was deep even at low tide. There they cast anchor and prepared to make themselves at home in the New World Leif had led them to.

That first night Leif spent ashore he never forgot. Tyrker had taken two men and gone hunting. He came back with a deer. Brendan had set other men to fishing in the river. They caught three enormous salmon, salmon bigger than they had ever seen. They built a huge fire and roasted the venison and fish and ate their fill of the good fresh food they'd been longing for.

As darkness fell—much earlier than the men were used to it in Greenland summers—a chorus of birds sang in the trees over their heads and an enormous moon swam slowly up the sky. Leif sat up by the dying fire, his hands clasped about his knees, too happy to sleep. At last the birds were silent, all was still, and only a fragrance of pine and sea freshness mingled in the air. Leif stretched out his arms and lay back.

"Brendan," he said.

Brendan gave a sleepy grunt.

"If the Irish came here," Leif told him, "it's no wonder they stayed."

CHAPTER IX

Vineland the Good

THE FIRST THING LEIF AND HIS PARTY DID WAS
to make sure of shelter. It did not take long to
build sleeping quarters, but Leif had his men fell
trees all about their camp to the distance of a bowshot. He had seen no men, no evidence of men, but
that did not mean there *were* no men in this paradise. He did not intend to allow any enemy to creep
up on his camp unseen and unheard. Everyone approaching must come either across the lake or
across a wide cleared space on shore.

It was not really the Irish he expected to find nor, he thought, did Brendan really expect to either. This land was so enormous, just the part they'd seen so far, that Leif knew the chances were very small of stumbling on the traces of any earlier party of settlers. But what stuck in his mind were the skin boats and the stone axes that the Greenlanders had found in their own country. He had always believed them to be relics of primitive people native to Greenland. Where had those people come from? Where had they gone to?

We know now that the Eskimos had, at that time, withdrawn far to the north in Greenland, leaving it almost empty. Men who have studied the subject believe that this was because the climate in Greenland was milder when Eric settled there than it is today, when Eskimos live all around the coast of Greenland. Eskimos need a cold climate, for they are used to living on Arctic animals. In pursuit of the game they were used to, then, they had moved out of southern Greenland.

Not for many years did they come into contact with the Norse settlers. Then it was the Norse, hunting farther and farther to the north, who stumbled on the Eskimos, not the Eskimos who found the Norse.

Leif, of course, knew nothing of this, but he did know that unknown men had lived at one time in Greenland. It seemed most likely that, if they had lived in Greenland, they had lived also in this much richer land. Why should they not live here still? In the virgin forests it was impossible to find traces of them, except by chance.

But Leif took no chances. His camp faced the woods across a space that his men could command with bows and spears. He kept a constant watch, and in his explorations he was careful to keep his camp always guarded by a party strong enough to hold it.

While they were building their houses and clearing the land, Leif sent the Irish runners out. They had a hard time in the heavily wooded country about, for it was not the kind of land where they could move fast. After a week or two Leif decided to use them only as advance scouts for a stronger body of men.

The two runners reported, through Brendan, that there were no traces of inhabitants for a day's journey anywhere about the camp, but Leif continued to be watchful.

When the wooden huts had been made strong and secure, Leif divided his men into two groups. The first stayed by the settlement, fishing, setting traps, smoking fish and meat for the winter supplies they would need, and keeping a guard on ship and on shore. The second group went exploring. With axes and knives they hacked their way through the woodland, the Irish runners moving ahead to serve, as Brendan had said, as eyes and ears.

Sometimes Leif went with the explorers. At other times he stayed in camp to supervise the work there while Brendan took command of the men spying out the land. They had arrived too late in the year to plant any crops, but Leif could see that the land would bear well. The soil was rich, the growing season much longer than even in Norway. Wheat, which they could not grow at all in Greenland, would do well here. And as for cattle, they could grow fat on rich pasture land for months longer than in the north.

Leif dreamed many dreams as he moved about his work. Why should he not return with a party of colonists to settle here, as his father had settled

Greenland? How much better and richer life could be here than in the north where just to stay alive was a struggle! They had gone hungry in Brattah-lid some winters after a bad season. No one who worked the land and planned ahead need ever go hungry here. Of course, they were thousands of miles from the wealth and the products of Norway, but that was true of Greenland too.

Food crops would grow here, cattle and sheep would thrive, wool could be woven, fuel was plentiful. Of course, they would need iron for tools and weapons. But why should they not find that here, too, and set up their own smithies?

If only the land was as empty as it seemed! If only they would not have to fight for it with other men! Each time that Leif went exploring he rejoiced anew over the emptiness as well as the richness of the country. Each time that he waited in camp he was again relieved to hear from the returning party that no inhabitants had been discovered and that all the men had come back safe.

And then one day Tyrker, of all people, disappeared! Canny, wise old Tyrker who had come to keep an eye on the young men, Tyrker who was quite as pleased as Leif that no native had been seen, was missing. Some of the younger men quite frankly longed for a bit of excitement and hoped for the discovery of something or someone, whether it were men or monsters. But Tyrker had grunted his contempt at this desire for excitement. He said that he had enough to keep him entertained without coming upon trolls, giants, or creatures who hopped on one leg and carried their heads under their arms. For Tyrker to disappear was beyond belief!

Leif was very angry. He gave a tongue-lashing to all the men who returned without Tyrker, not sparing Brendan. How could they have lost the old man? Had no one been close to him? Had no one heard him call? When had they seen him last?

Brendan, who had borne Leif's anger quietly, said, "It was after lunch. We stopped on the bank of a stream to cook some fish and he was with us as we started back. But we had to string out a bit to follow the trail through a patch of thick forest and—he was gone. But if you ask me——"

"I didn't ask you!" Leif shouted. Then he swallowed and said, "All right, Brendan. What?"

"He went off for some reason of his own. He's had something up his sleeve for the last week. He's disappeared a couple of times before for an hour or so——"

"Why didn't you tell me that?" Leif asked.

"Because he always turned up," Brendan replied. "And it was close to the camp that he did it. He could always find his own way back. Even to-day——"

"Today *I'm* going to look for him. You and your men can stay here and keep guard." Leif called a dozen men who had been in camp all day. They got ready quickly, for it would be dusk in an hour or so, and they started out calling as they went, then pausing to listen for an answering shout. The Irish runners went ahead to retrace the path they had traveled. On and on they went while the shadows grew longer. Leif was just about to give up, fearing to lose himself and his search party in the dark.

Then out of the woods to the right, with a crackling of twigs, came a figure.

"Tyrker!" shouted Leif. The men halted and the ones ahead turned back. Leif ran to the old man and took him in his arms. "Tyrker, foster-father, where have you been? What's kept you out so late? It's nearly dark!"

It was Tyrker, all right—but when Leif let him

go and looked at him he felt his heart sink into his boots. Tyrker's eyes rolled in his head, he hit Leif smartly on the shoulder, gave a roar of laughter, and burst into speech in a tongue Leif could not understand!

"He's enchanted!" one of the search party cried, and the men huddled close about Leif, peering over their shoulders at the twilight forest.

"Take him back to camp," Leif said grimly. He wouldn't admit it to the men, but enchantment did seem the only possible reason for Tyrker's behavior. Two of the men started to pick up Tyrker to carry him home.

The old man struggled madly in their arms. "Nein! Nein!" he shouted and, breaking away, dashed back into the trees. Heartsick, Leif crashed after him.

He almost fell over him. Tyrker had stopped and was trying to pick up a big wooden cask. As Leif paused, Tryker turned to him waving his arms, still talking his strange language. But after a moment he passed his hand over his face and spoke at last in Norse.

"Leif, my good boy, look what I've made! Here, take a drink!" He waved at the cask.

Out of the woods came Tyrker

Leif shook his head firmly. Whatever had enchanted Tyrker, Leif wasn't going to drink any.

"I'm not enchanted," Tyrker said, and began to laugh. He took Leif's arm and hung on to it. "But I'm very much afraid, my boy, that I am a little drunk!"

"Drunk!"

"It's a lot stronger than I thought! Leif, go on, taste it—just a drop! It's wine, Leif, it's wine! I made it!"

"Wine!"

"Certainly, wine." Tyrker stood up straighter and groaned. "But it's stronger than I expected. Here, get some of the men to carry it. I intended to bring it into camp all by myself as a surprise, but I had to sample it to see if it was ready to drink and —well——"

"You took a sample that was a little too big!" Leif began to laugh. "Oh, foster-father, wait until I tell Eric how wisely and well you looked after the young men! Reeling about the forest, shouting—what were you shouting?"

"German, naturally," said Tyrker, trying to regain his dignity. "It's my native tongue, isn't it? Where did I learn to make wine but in Germany?

So when I think of wine, I think in German. Not in Norse, not in the language of men who know nothing about wine, don't even know grapes when they see them! The woods are full of wild grapes, Leif, wherever there's a bit of a clearing. I've been watching them ripen for a month, and for a week I've had this nice little brew fermenting——"

"And you've gone off every now and then to see if it was ready."

"How did you know that?" Tyrker asked. "Brendan, I suppose. I thought he had his eye on me."

"A good thing he did, too," Leif exclaimed. "Or you'd never have got back to camp, you drunken old man! I'm ashamed of you!"

"Laugh if you want," said Tyrker. "But without me you'd never have known there were wine grapes here."

"That I wouldn't," said Leif, still laughing. He called the men and they returned to camp. Tyrker went promptly to sleep, and Leif portioned out the wine carefully so that everyone had a small drink with the evening meal. But Tyrker's misadventure made Leif very careful to keep the drinks small!

Next day he set his men, under Tyrker's direction, to gathering grapes. He allowed Tyrker to
make a little wine, for he knew they might need it
to warm them occasionally during the winter. But
most of the grapes he had dried into raisins for
transport back to Greenland.

When the grape season was over, Leif had grapevines cut. Hempen rope was unknown, walrus-hide
rope expensive. For many purposes the tough
grapevines would take the place of rope.

Leif was delighted with Tyrker's discovery, and
he named the country Vineland. So it was known
for centuries, in Icelandic sagas and in the annals
of the Catholic Church.

The winter amazed them by its warmth and by
the height of the sun. The saga writer recorded,
and it is still there to be read, Leif's astonishment
at having breakfast in full daylight. Compared to
Greenland it almost seemed as if cattle could pasture out all winter. There was plenty of game all
winter, too.

It was even more amazing that not once did Leif
and his party see another human being. And yet,
Leif did not believe the land vacant. It was too rich,
too good. Sometimes he had a feeling that some-

thing, someone, was watching. Never, therefore, did he relax the care with which a guard was kept. Perhaps it was just this care that kept him from seeing Vineland's inhabitants.

Then it was spring, and time to go. As trees came into bud and wild flowers bloomed, Leif prepared to sail back to Greenland. His cargo was timber, grape vines and dried grapes—so many that they loaded the ship's boat full and towed her astern.

On the return trip, they followed the same course by which they had come. Sailing along the coast, Leif noted every landmark for later trips. At length, when the wooded shores gave place to barren ones, Leif left the land and struck for home across Davis Strait. He had a fair wind and it was not many days before he saw the Greenland glaciers before him.

The land was so clear that Leif and Brendan were already discussing their exact whereabouts. They had just decided they were farther north than the settlement when Leif, at the helm, changed his course.

"What's the matter?" Brendan asked. "You're coming into the wind too much."

"I'm watching the wind," Leif said. "But I'm

watching something else, too. What do you see that's strange?"

Brendan squinted and looked, but could see nothing. "You've got better eyes than I have. What is it?"

"A ship—or a reef. I don't know which." Leif called to the men to be ready to let the sail down and get the oars out.

After a few minutes Brendan said, "It's a reef."

"Yes, it's a reef, I think. But there are men on it."

"I can't see them," Brendan said.

"You will." They drew closer rapidly. "Down with the sail there!" Leif shouted. The ship lost speed, the oars came out, and cautiously they crept up to a tiny rocky island.

The party of people marooned on the reef were waving and shouting. Two of them climbed to the top of a pile of timber and waved furiously. Their voices came faintly across the waves. "Ship-wrecked!" they called. "We've been shipwrecked! Help! Help!"

Several of Leif's men pulled the small boat in under the stern and loaded most of the cargo they had carried there from Vineland onto the larger vessel.

"Take the boat, Tyrker," said Leif, "and get them off."

Tyrker and two other men tumbled down into the remains of the vines and grapes in the boat and rowed to the island. Leif could hear Tyrker shouting, "Who's your captain?" But the waves drowned the answer. The boat danced about on the sea and it was no easy job to get the shipwrecked party into it. Tyrker had to make three trips.

As the first boatload came aboard, Leif went forward to meet them. To his astonishment, one of them was a woman. A tall thin man, shivering with cold, helped her up on to the ship. "I'm the captain," he said. "Thori, from Norway. This is my wife, Gudrid. Thank you, thank you a thousand times. We've been there for two days and we thought——Never mind what we thought. Who are you?"

"They call me Leif the Lucky. I think I'm lucky for you, today, as well as for myself."

"Are you the son of Eric the Red, of Brattah-lid?" Thori asked. "That's where we were bound, with a cargo of timber from Norway. We'll be glad enough to get there ourselves, let me tell you." Thori rubbed his chest and began to cough.

"You're soaked," Leif said. "Brendan, there are dry clothes under the after deck. Give these people what they need."

Thori and Gudrid went aft.

Leif stood staring with narrowed eyes at the coastline, making a mental picture of the landmarks. Then he went back to the helm. "I think we can save the timber later," he told Thori, "if we don't get a storm bad enough to wash it off. I'll remember this spot."

"So shall I," said Thori, "but not pleasantly. If you can get the timber off you're entitled to it." He began to cough again and Leif made him lie down after he had been wrapped in dry cloaks. Gudrid sat beside him. She was astonishingly beautiful.

There were fifteen people in all rescued from the reef. Leif made for home as quickly as he could, for all of them had suffered from exposure and Thori was really sick.

Two days later Ericsfiord opened before them, and Leif stood in for Brattahlid. He was home from the wilderness, home with a rich cargo and another waiting to be picked up off the reef. He was home with news of a paradise to the west. Leif the Lucky!

CHAPTER X

"Greenland Is My Home"

ERIC WAS DEAD. LEIF'S MOTHER MET HIM WITH
the news as he landed. His oldest brother, Thorvald, was with her. It was really he who told Leif,
for Thjodhild could hardly talk for weeping.

"Mother, Mother," Leif said, stroking her hair
and trying to comfort her. At last he said, "Mother,
I've brought guests! Poor shipwrecked folk from
Norway that we took off a reef to the north of here,
two days ago. One of them's sick and one's a

woman. Won't you make them welcome and take them to Brattahlid?"

It was the best thing he could have done. With someone else to worry about, Thjodhild at once became calmer. With Leif's other brother, Thorstein, she went to the ship and hurried Gudrid and Thori and their men up to the farm where they could be looked after.

Thorvald and Leif stood watching the men make the ship fast. They would begin unloading her tomorrow. Tonight they would feast and rest. "You found a rich land," Thorvald said.

"Yes," Leif answered.

"Will you go back?"

Leif looked up at Brattahlid above them and the wild naked mountains behind it. How different it was from the magnificent rich country where he had been! Yet, with Eric dead, it was his—his responsibility. How could he leave it? How could he leave his mother, and all the people who looked to the Master of Brattahlid as their chief? And yet— Vineland the Good! He did not answer Thorvald but said instead, "Tell me about my father."

"He aged after you went," Thorvald began, as if he were trying to remember each detail. "He took care of his ankle, and he stayed in bed for a month. Then he got up and began to hobble about the farm with a stick. He'd got very thin. I think it was then I began to know—when I saw how thin he was. He seemed not to be interested in anything. Thorhall had to come and ask him for orders to go north for the hunting. He'd forgotten all about it."

Thorvald turned to look at his brother. "He never talked much about you, Leif, but in the autumn he'd stand by the house and look west, as if he were watching for a ship. I told him once you planned to winter in the new country if you could and he said angrily, 'Of course he does. Do you take me for a fool?' But he watched for you, all the same.

"Then, just after Christmas—we thought he'd just caught a cold. But it got worse and worse and he got weaker and weaker. We couldn't seem to keep him warm. Finally one night he said, 'Look after things till Leif comes back.' I tried to say he'd be looking after them himself, but he answered 'Don't talk nonsense.' Then it was as if he wandered in his mind. He thought he was back in Iceland, and swore at the men who'd had him outlawed. Toward the end he was quiet and when he talked he seemed to be having a long conversation with the old god Thor."

"Then he died?" said Leif.

"Just like that. In his sleep. He's buried on the hill behind the farm, looking west to the sea and beyond."

"That was right," said Leif. Then they went up to the house.

All summer long, as Leif ran the farm, he struggled within himself to know what to do. In the end he realized that he was struggling against what he had to do. He had to stay home. He had had two great voyages, to Norway and to Vineland. How could he ask his brothers to stay at home and run the farm for him while he went adventuring? It would not be fair. So when, that winter, Thorvald asked him again if he was going back to Vineland, he said "No."

Thorvald sat silent for a long time. At last he said, "If I had your ship——"

"It's yours," said Leif.

So in the spring Thorvald sailed for Vineland. With Leif's directions to follow he found the very place where Leif had made camp. Leif had explored closely around the settlement and it seemed to Thorvald that it would be wise to go farther afield.

He took the ship's boat and a small party of men and they went on a long trip west along the shore. From the description that has come down to us, it seems likely that this trip was made along the southern coast of Cape Cod, Rhode Island and Connecticut. They saw no men, but they found a queer conical structure at one place that they took to be a storage bin for grain. But it is as likely that it was an empty bark tepee. They knew, at any rate, that it had been built by men, and they returned thoughtfully to camp.

Thorvald and his men wintered in Leif's camp and the next summer explored the land to the east and north in the ship. They had bad luck here. A storm came up suddenly—most likely one of the wicked northeasters that plague the New England coast—and the ship ran aground on a projecting headland and broke her keel. It took them some time to make a new keel and repair the ship. When they had finished, Thorvald had the men set up the old keel as a kind of monument, or landmark, and they named the place Keel Cape.

Rounding the cape, they sailed east again, going

into several bays. At one place a beautiful wooded headland ran out into the sea.

"That's the place for me," said Thorvald. "Here I should like to stay."

They landed and made a short journey of exploration. When they came down to the beach again the men in the lead stopped suddenly. On the shore were three queer lumps. Cautiously they approached. Under three skin canoes nine men were sleeping! Here were the first of the savage inhabitants of Vineland to be seen by the Norse!

The savages leapt up, to find themselves surrounded by tall blond men in armor, with swords and spears. Grasping their canoes, the savages tried to turn them over and get them into the water.

"Don't let them escape!" cried Thorvald. "They'll bring their companions down on us!" Swords came out, spears flew and in a moment the beach was reddened by savage blood. But one of the Indians—or Skraelings, as the Norse called them —slipped through their hands and got his canoe into the water. Spears and arrows did not stop him. Kneeling and paddling at incredible speed, he was soon out of bowshot.

"This is a bad day's work," said Thorvald.

"Bury the dead men quickly so they will not be found. Then we must go up to the headland and try to see if we can discover from where an attack might come." When they reached this vantage point, they saw, in a valley behind, a group of mounds which they thought might be the savages' homes.

"We'd best get back to the ship," said Thorvald and they panted down to the beach again. But Thorvald had wasted too much time. From behind the headland a canoe came flying and then another and another.

"Quick, out to the ship," shouted Thorvald. They were ranging shields along the side as a protection against arrows when a mass of canoes, too many to be counted, was upon them, and a flight of arrows struck the ship.

"Up with the anchor!" shouted Thorvald. "Out oars!" Swiftly they rowed out.

The canoes followed them a little way, still shooting; but not for long. Suddenly sea and land were as bare of savages as ever.

Thorvald at the steering oar called out, "Anyone hurt?"

After a moment the answer came back, "No!"

Thorvald raised his arm. "I am." The men saw an arrow in his side. "This thing came in between the shield and the gunwale." Two men came to him quickly to try to get it out. "Don't," said Thorvald. "It will kill me fast enough as it is. Don't open the wound to get it out." He paused. One of the men took the steering oar.

Thorvald leaned back. "Do this," he said. "Get out of here and go home as quick as you can. But I would like to be buried on that headland where I said I would like to stay. That was the truth I spoke when I said I would stay there awhile! Put a cross at my head and call it Cross Cape." His head fell forward on his chest and he spoke no more.

The next day, the savages having withdrawn as quickly as they had come, Thorvald was buried as he had asked to be. His men went back to Leif's camp and gathered vines and grapes for their cargo, and next spring they returned to Greenland with the news of Thorvald's death.

Nor was this all Leif and his mother had had to bear. Leif's other brother, Thorstein, was dead too. A disease had come to Greenland with a ship from Norway, and Thorstein and many others of the colony had died the past winter.

The woman Gudrid, whom Leif had rescued from the reef, had been married briefly to Thorstein before he died. Her first husband, Thori, had never recovered from the shipwreck. After he died, Thorstein had pressed her to marry him and about a year later she did. Now she was a widow twice over, though still young and beautiful. She was a great comfort to Leif's mother Thjodhild. Many men in Greenland would have liked to marry her, but she shook her head and smiled and would not. She stayed at Brattahlid helping Thjodhild with the running of the house, the weaving and sewing.

But Gudrid did marry again, and she was the first Norsewoman to go to Vineland. It happened this way. Leif had been too busy even to think of Vineland again. Deaths from disease had weakened the Greenland colony. Those men who were left worked very hard to keep their flocks fed and to get in a sufficient supply of food for the winter. Leif was bound to Brattahlid and could not leave.

Late one summer two ships came to Greenland from Iceland, under the command of a man named Thorfinn whose nickname was Karlsefni. This means "stuff of a man"—that is, Thorfinn "Who is just what a man should be," or in slang, Thor-finn "Who is quite a guy"! Karlsefni and his companions had come to trade, and Leif was very glad to have their supplies landed, for Greenland needed them badly. He invited Karlsefni to stay at Brattahlid that winter with all his men.

Leif liked Karlsefni at once. The Icelander was not only brave but he seemed to be wise, sensible, and a fine commander as well. When Leif was worried about supplies for the traditional Christmas feast, Karlsefni quietly had food brought from his ships and insisted that Leif use it.

During the long winter nights Leif found himself telling his guest about Vineland. Karlsefni was deeply interested and it seemed to Leif that he was interested in the right way. He thought of Vineland not just as a place to go for an adventure, and to bring home a good cargo, but as a land in which the Norse might settle permanently. This had been Leif's dream too.

"Why don't you try it, Thorfinn?" Leif said one night.

Karlsefni looked at him. "It was your discovery, Leif. It should be you who goes."

"Greenland is my home," Leif said. "I can't

leave. The colony was weakened by disease and I must see that it is strengthened again. But you can go."

"I would want to take a strong party," Karlsefni said thoughtfully. "I would like to try to make a permanent settlement, as Eric did here. I would want to take women as well as men." After a moment he added, "I would particularly like to take your sister-in-law Gudrid as my wife."

"That's up to Gudrid," Leif told him. "Since my brother died she has refused many offers to marry."

"I know that," said Karlsefni. "But if she agreed you would not object?"

"If she asks me, I shall urge her to do it. And I urge you to sail for Vineland. You shall have the Irish runners that King Olaf gave me to help in your explorations, and Tyrker, who was with me ——No, Tyrker is getting old and I need him here. And Brendan, who sailed with me, plans a trading voyage to Ireland in the spring for goods we sorely need here. But Thorhall the Huntsman would be useful to you, and I can spare him."

"You're too generous, Leif."

Leif shook his head. "No. I want you to be successful. Every man and woman I can spare without weakening Greenland further is free to go with you."

They settled it between them that night. The next day Gudrid came to Leif and told him that Karlsefni had asked her to marry him, and had told her of his plan to sail for Vineland.

"You would be a help to him," Leif said. "He is a very good man. I think you should do it."

Then Gudrid told Leif that before Thorstein had died, he had told her that she was not to marry another Greenlander, but that she would marry an Icelander, have many adventures and a long life, and leave behind her descendants who would be powerful and famous.

"He may have been raving in delirium, of course," she finished, "but it didn't seem like that. He spoke quite clearly. He said he was so near death that he could see into the future——I don't know what to believe. But at any rate, Leif, whether Thorstein foretold the future or not, Thorfinn Karlsefni is the man I would like to marry, if Thjodhild can get on without me here."

"Of course we will get on," Leif said to her.

Leif and Karlsefni discussed plans for the voyage again and again and in the spring Karlsefni sailed with a party of one hundred and sixty men and women. Among them were Gudrid and Leif's sister Freydis, for she and her husband Thorvard added their own ship to Karlsefni's two.

CHAPTER XI

Karlsefni's Voyage

KARLSEFNI DID NOT FOLLOW LEIF'S ROUTE TO Vineland. Leif and Thorvald had each had only one ship, but Karlsefni had three and had to think about keeping his party together. He sailed north, therefore, which seems an odd thing to do if you want to go southwest, but it really was sensible. This route brought him to where Davis Strait is narrower and where his crossing of the open sea, which had taken Bjarni four days and Leif six, was cut down to two.

Thorhall the Huntsman had advised that this route be used. He knew more about the northernmost lands and waters than anyone else in Greenland for he had hunted to the north every summer of the twenty that the Norse had been in Greenland.

The land Karlsefni found first was just as Leif had described it, barren and covered with flat stones. Karlsefni, having looked it over briefly, went on south. He came to the forested country that Leif had named Markland and sailed on past.

We hear next of the long sandy beaches his party skirted before they found a coastline indented with bays where they dropped anchor. Karlsefni set the runners ashore and they were gone for three days. When they came back they reported (they had learned a bit of the Norse language by now) that the land seemed good. Karlsefni decided to make camp.

Was this the same region that Leif and Thorvald had explored? It seems doubtful. Karlsefni's party experienced a much more bitter winter than the mild weather that Leif had known. It was more open country, for we hear not of woods, but of grass and rugged hills. The game animals left the region in the winter and food grew very scarce.

Karlsefni had four times as many people to provide supplies for as Leif had had, and some of them were women. Before the winter passed they were almost starving. The weather was too severe for them to fish from small boats and they were reduced to hunting along the shore and on a nearby island for something—anything—washed ashore that might be edible.

At this point old Thorhall the Huntsman went off by himself, and they didn't find him for three days. It was his business to hunt, of course, but why should he have gone alone? It was Karlsefni and a man named Bjarni Grimulfsson who found him at last, lying on top of a steep cliff, staring up at the sky and mumbling strange words while he pinched and scratched at himself.

When Karlsefni and Bjarni asked him what he was doing, he told them to mind their business— he'd lived long enough to need no help from the likes of them! Karlsefni wondered whether Thorhall might not have gone a little mad from hunger. At any rate, he at last agreed to go back to the camp, and they helped him down the cliff.

The next day a dead whale was blown ashore. The hungry men fell on the carcass ravenously, cut up the meat and cooked it. Karlsefni had done a great deal of whaling, but even he didn't know what kind it was. This, however, did not stop the starving men from gorging on whale flesh.

Thorhall was particularly happy. He burst out finally with the news that the whale was the answer to his prayers. He'd gone up on the cliff to pray to Thor and make magic, and in return the whale had been sent! "Was not red-bearded Thor more helpful than your God?" he shouted at the men about him. Unfortunately for Thor's reputation, the whale meat made everybody sick!

This was the worst time they had; but in a few days the weather improved and Karlsefni ordered men out to fish in small boats. They had a good catch, and after that they had enough to eat.

As spring came on, Karlsefni talked over plans with the other men in the party. He wanted to sail south, in search of the mild winters and the rich grape-bearing country that Leif had told him of.

Everyone agreed, except stubborn old Thorhall. He was sure that Karlsefni had somehow sailed too far and missed Vineland, and that it was necessary to go north to find it. Karlsefni argued with him, but Thorhall was convinced that he was right. In the end he persuaded nine men to his point of view. Karlsefni would not let him have a ship—Thorhall's party could not have manned it, anyway—but he gave him an eight-oared boat, the largest of the ship's boats.

Thorhall went off with his supporters, shouting verses back at Karlsefni to the effect that he had not come to Vineland to drink water and eat whale meat! He did not find Vineland—for he was blown clear across the Atlantic to Ireland by a stiff gale! When he and his party landed, the Irish swiftly enslaved them.

Fortunately Brendan, who had been trading in Ireland, heard a report of their arrival and hastened down to help them. He bought Thorhall and his men free, but the old man had suffered terribly on the awful sea-crossing in an open boat, and he did not live to see Greenland again.

In the meantime Karlsefni, Bjarni Grimulfsson, Snorri Thorbrandsson, Freydis, and her husband

Thorvard sailed south. They came at last to country as rich as that which Leif had found. It may very well have been even farther to the south, some think as far south as Georgia. Grapes grew in abundance on the high ground, and wild grain on the lower land. They caught fish simply by digging pits in the sand of the beaches, where the fish were stranded as the tide went out. Many kinds of animals could be found in the woods. There was a fine protected anchorage for their ships in a bay behind a sand bar.

Here they settled and began to build houses. Leif had told Karlsefni of the precautions he had taken to prevent enemy savages from creeping up on his camp. But Karlsefni had visitors before he had a chance to make himself secure! Early one morning the Norsemen saw nine canoes paddling toward them. The Skraelings, as they called the Indians, were coming!

Everyone knew, of course, how Thorvald had died from a Skraeling arrow. But that was after Thorvald's men had killed eight of the savages in cold blood.

"We will have no fighting if we can help it!" Karlsefni told his men. He ordered the women to hide in the half-built houses. Then, encouraged by the fact that this seemed to be too small a party of savages to have come with unfriendly intentions, he went down to the water's edge to greet them.

The Skraelings drove their canoes on to the beach with powerful strokes of the paddle, and leapt ashore. Wild men and Vikings stared at each other in astonishment. What the savages thought of the big blond men we do not know. But the Norsemen reported the Skraelings to be "dark men, ugly to look at. Their hair was unkempt; they had big eyes and broad cheeks." The savages stared about them, marveling.

Karlsefni tried to speak to the Skraelings, but they did not answer. They made no move to fight, and Karlsefni kept his men back from pressing too close about them. Suddenly, at a gesture from their leader, they jumped into their canoes and paddled away.

Though the savages had been peaceful, Karlsefni was worried. He hurried on the building of the houses, and he had the men set a strong stockade wall of heavy logs about them. He had special reasons of his own for wanting his party safe, for that autumn his wife Gudrid gave birth to a son

Karlsefni and his men chased the

Skraelings to the water's edge . . .

named Snorri. It was the first white child born on the North American continent! But for the rest of that year and through the winter the Skraelings did not come. No snow fell that winter, and the cattle that the settlers had brought were out at pasture right through the coldest months.

Then in the early spring the savages returned. There was a great number of them this time, canoe after canoe after canoe. With shields on their arms and spears in their hands the Norsemen awaited their coming, knowing full well that if it should come to a fight, they were badly outnumbered.

But the Skraelings had come to trade. Each man carried a quantity of furs with him, and offered them to the Vikings. The closest they came to trouble was when a tall savage laid his hand on Karlsefni's sword. Karlsefni removed the hand gently and shook his head. The savage held out his whole supply of furs, offering them in exchange for the sword. But Karlsefni did not allow any weapons to be traded. Even if the Norsemen could have spared them, they did not dare let the Skraelings take possession of iron swords and spears.

Karlsefni soon discovered that bright red cloth pleased the savages just as much as weapons. The

Skraelings were delighted to get strips of it, which they tied about their heads.

It was not a quarrel that put an end to the bargaining, but the Vikings' bull! The cattle had been out of sight when the Skraelings landed, but now the bull ran out of the woods bellowing furiously. The savages broke and ran in terror before this monstrous beast, the like of which they had never seen before. They took to the canoes in panic and vanished to the south along the coast.

Three weeks later they came back, and this time they howled as they came. For the first time the dreaded Indian war-whoop fell upon the ears of men from the Old World. There was no doubt this time that the Skraelings intended war.

The Norsemen went out to meet them while the women huddled inside the stockade. A furious flight of arrows greeted them but their armor protected them.

The savages proved to have an even more terrible weapon—a huge rock wrapped in leather that was hurled through the air by a kind of sling-shot arrangement. The Skraelings launched this missile at the closely grouped men and felled two of them.

Meanwhile other Skraelings thronged about the stockade where the women were gathered. Gudrid clasped her baby to her breast and prayed aloud for aid. Not so Freydis, Leif's sister. She was a true daughter of Eric the Red! The savages were battering the door of the stockade open when Freydis ran to meet them. Outside lay a dead Viking, cut down as he tried to hold the Skraelings away from the door. Freydis caught up his sword and as the savages rushed the open door, they found Freydis waiting for them in the gap.

"If the men have run," she cried, "the women can fight too!" They did not understand her of course, but even savages could hear the passion in her voice. They stopped. Freydis stroked the sword across her breast as if she were whetting the blade on her body, and in the face of danger and death, she laughed aloud!

At the sound, the Skraelings tumbled back against each other and fled as they had fled from the bellowing bull!

In a moment the Norsemen followed, pursuing the fleeing savages. One of the Skraelings was not too terrified to pause and pick up an iron axe with which a Norseman had been chopping wood when the alarm came. He tried it on the wood and seemed to think it marvelous. Then he swung it at a rock. Nothing happened, except that the edge of the axe blade was blunted. The savage threw it aside with a grunt and ran after his fellows.

Karlsefni and his men chased the Skraelings to the water's edge, where they went off as quickly as ever. Then the Norsemen came back to the women. Freydis was the heroine of the day.

That night Karlsefni called a council of war. Could they stay here, not knowing when howling wild men might sweep down on them? How could they work the land? Or go afield to hunt and fish? They had found a rich land but, as Thorvard said, "How long are we likely to enjoy it?" The savages vastly outnumbered them. They had been frightened off twice, but the Vikings could not count on that happening again.

At last they all agreed that they could not stay in this earthly paradise where everything welcomed them except the men who dwelt there. It was a sad time they had in the next few weeks, loading their ships for departure and bidding farewell to this spot that they had hoped to make their home.

They did not return at once to Greenland, for

Karlsefni felt he must look for Thorhall and his party. So they followed the land north, and spent another winter in the rougher, more northerly climate where they had first stopped. They were careful to lay in enough supplies, and no one went hungry that winter. But of course they found no traces of Thorhall. At length, their ships loaded with furs, grapes, vines, and timber, they set sail for Greenland.

Leif welcomed them with joy and Karlsefni and Gudrid spent the winter with him before they went on to Iceland. Through the long nights Leif and Karlsefni talked often of Vineland and of how—someday—a colony of brave men might settle there. But though ships sailed from Greenland to Markland for timber as long as the Greenland colony lasted, the Vikings were never able to establish a settlement on the American continent.

It was not until five hundred years later that the superior weapons of the Spaniards were able to keep the savages at bay. With only swords, spears and arrows the fearless Norsemen did not have a chance against the wild men who outnumbered them.

But the discovery of Vineland the Good was

never wholly forgotten. Sixty-odd years after Karlsefni's voyage, in 1070, Adam of Bremen set down the first brief written record of "an island in the ocean called Vineland" which he had heard about from the Danish King. In Greenland and in Iceland the stories of Leif's voyage and Karlsefni's attempt at settlement were told and retold, and recorded as we have them now sometime in the eleven hundreds.

The little boy Snorri who was born in Vineland left a long line of famous descendants who loved to tell of their ancestors' adventures.

Most interesting of all—Ferdinand Columbus, who wrote the life of his father, says that Christopher Columbus went to Iceland in 1476 or 1477. Who knows what stories Columbus may not have heard there of rich lands to the west, beyond the sea?